# 77
*fairly safe*
# SCIENCE
## ACTIVITIES
*for illustrating*
# BIBLE
## LESSONS

# 77

*fairly safe*

# SCIENCE
## ACTIVITIES
*for illustrating*
# BIBLE
## LESSONS

## Donald B. DeYoung

BakerBooks

*a division of Baker Publishing Group*
Grand Rapids, Michigan

Published by Baker Books
a division of Baker Publishing Group
P.O. Box 6287, Grand Rapids, MI 49516-6287
www.bakerbooks.com

Many of the activities were previously published by Baker in *Science and the Bible*, volumes 1–3 (1994, 1997, 2002) by Donald B. DeYoung

Printed in the United States of America

Library of Congress Cataloging-in-Publication Data
DeYoung, Donald B.
    77 fairly safe science activities for illustrating Bible lessons / Donald B.
DeYoung.
        pages cm
    ISBN 978-0-8010-1537-3 (pbk.)
        1. Bible and science—Miscellanea. 2. Christian education—Activity programs.
    I. Title. II. Title: Seventy-seven fairly safe science activities for illustrating Bible
lessons.
    BS650.D48  2013
    268′.6—dc23                                                          2013016848

18   19        7   6   5

# Contents

# List of Lesson Activities and Themes

1. The actual size of the sun is measured with a ruler.
   Gen. 1:16—The sun displays God's majesty.
2. The design of a feather is explored.
   Gen. 1:20—Feathers show God's design.
3. Acids and bases are distinguished.
   Gen. 1:28—The universe is orderly.
4. A mixture of salt and ice results in a very low temperature.
   Gen. 2:1—God's laws are dependable.
5. An artificial tree is made from paper.
   Gen. 2:9—Creation is to be enjoyed.
6. Sound vibrations are made visible.
   Gen. 4:21—Music is a gift from God.
7. A map is cut out to show continental separation.
   Gen. 7:11—The Genesis flood was worldwide.
8. Colors are separated from light using a CD or DVD.
   Gen. 9:13—Believing God's promises
9. Sand grains are counted.
   Gen. 22:17—God's family is large and growing.

10. A stairway is built from blocks.

     Gen. 28:12—We are always in touch with heaven.

11. An electric circuit is completed to light a bulb.

     Exod. 9:16—Using God's resources

12. Crystals are grown on a rock surface.

     Num. 17:8—God makes a garden grow.

13. Paper loops make unusual shapes.

     Deut. 29:29—God tells us what we need to know about life.

14. Various liquids and solids are mixed.

     2 Kings 6:6—God has power over nature.

15. A magnetic field is made visible.

     2 Kings 6:17—Realizing God's power

16. Copper is plated onto a nail.

     2 Kings 6:17—A host of angels defends the believer.

17. Light sticks are compared with fireflies.

     Job 12:7–8—Creation teaches practical lessons.

18. Cans are crushed by the pressure of air.

     Job 28:24–25—Believing the Bible

19. Water glasses are made to ring.

     Job 35:10—Resting in the Lord

20. A magnifying lens is made with a water droplet.

     Job 36:24—Creation evidence is always before our eyes.

21. Ink is added to water.

     Job 37:13—God controls the weather.

22. Numbers in nature are explored.

     Job 38:4—Created patterns show God's fingerprint.

23. Sticks are balanced on one's fingers.

     Ps. 16:8—God provides stability in a changing world.

24. Light is separated into colors.

     Ps. 19:1—God's colorful artwork fills the skies.

25. The elliptical paths of planets are drawn.

     Ps. 19:1—Planets obey God's laws of motion.

26. A volunteer is tied up with tape.

    Ps. 19:12–13—Forming good habits

27. One person wins a tug-of-war against several others.

    Ps. 46:1—Using God's resources

28. A lens is shown to invert objects.

    Ps. 94:9—Eyesight is a precious gift from God.

29. Paper is folded several times.

    Ps. 104:14—God cares for his creatures.

30. Sound is amplified with a pin and paper.

    Ps. 139:14—The gift of hearing

31. The sense of touch is explored.

    Prov. 3:5—We cannot always trust our own judgment.

32. Newspapers are torn in easy and difficult directions.

    Prov. 3:6—Choosing direction in life

33. The properties of carbon dioxide are shown.

    Prov. 14:12—The way to heaven

34. Eggs are safely tossed at a target.

    Prov. 15:1—Self-control

35. Air pressure is observed.

    Prov. 19:11—It pays to be patient.

36. Vinegar and baking soda make carbon dioxide gas.

    Prov. 19:19—Controlling temper

37. Raisins are made to rise and fall in liquid.

    Prov. 21:5—Seek the Lord's direction.

38. A bucket of water is safely swung in a circle.

    Prov. 29:25—Trusting in God

39. Groundwater is explored.

    Eccles. 1:7—God supplies our daily needs.

40. Construction paper is bleached to a white color.

    Isa. 1:18—God's forgiveness is complete.

41. A blind spot is demonstrated.

    Isa. 35:5—New life in Christ

42. A balloon is suspended in the air with a hair dryer.

   Isa. 40:31—Using the Lord's strength

43. The cooling effect of water is measured.

   Ezek. 34:26—The creative design of water

44. Boiled and fresh eggs are compared.

   Amos 3:3—Friendship with Christ

45. A stone and other objects are dissolved.

   Hab. 3:6—God outlasts the mountains.

46. A burning candle is sealed inside a glass.

   Matt. 5:15—The gospel must be shared.

47. A coin is dropped into a glass.

   Matt. 24:40–41—Trusting in the Lord

48. Soda cans are compared by weight.

   Matt. 25:32—God knows our hearts.

49. Water is made to swirl from one bottle to another.

   Mark 4:39—Turning to God

50. Creative designs are constructed.

   Mark 10:6—A special part of creation

51. Two plungers cannot be separated.

   Mark 10:27—God is able to save us.

52. A boiled egg is pushed into an empty bottle.

   Luke 11:24—Filling the heart with God

53. Eggshells support the weight of many books.

   Luke 12:6—God's tender care

54. Round and square shapes are compared.

   Luke 19:4—God designed trees with strength.

55. Two pendulums affect each other in a curious way.

   John 13:35—Giving help and encouragement

56. A single sheet of paper is cut to make a large doorway.

   John 20:19—Realizing God's presence

57. A downhill race is held between objects.

   1 Cor. 9:24—Be faithful to God.

58. The colors within ink are observed.

    1 Cor. 12:27—The church family

59. A mirror gives strange reflections.

    1 Cor. 13:12—Understanding God's plan

60. Rulers are dropped to measure short reaction times.

    1 Cor. 15:51–52—Accepting the Lord

61. The force of expanding seeds breaks a jar.

    2 Cor. 5:17—Sharing the gospel

62. Cotton is added to water.

    Eph. 3:20—God blesses us beyond our imaginations.

63. A ball is swung in a circle and released.

    Col. 1:17—A dependable universe

64. The apparent and actual depths of water are compared.

    Col. 3:20—Obey your parents.

65. Pepper spreads out on water.

    1 Tim. 6:11—Run from sin.

66. Surface tension of water is observed.

    Heb. 1:3—God holds the universe together.

67. One balloon is popped inside another.

    Heb. 4:12—Knowing ourselves

68. A comparison is made between hard water and soft water.

    Heb. 4:13—Looking on the inside

69. A banana is sliced without being peeled.

    Heb. 11:1—Understanding faith

70. A person swivels on a chair.

    Heb. 12:1—Dropping things that hinder

71. A form of Silly Putty is made from cornstarch.

    James 1:6, 8—An unstable person

72. An object floats or sinks in water.

    James 3:4–5—The power of the tongue must be used wisely.

73. A large object is moved with a small push.

    James 5:16—Prayer brings results.

74. Stalactites are grown.

    2 Pet. 3:8—Creation was recent.

75. Objects are balanced in unusual ways.

    2 Pet. 3:17—Keeping steady in the Lord

76. Water is separated into gases.

    Rev. 14:7—Water displays God's creative handiwork.

77. A sandwich bag is heated without melting.

    Rev. 22:17—Accepting the gift of salvation

# Introduction

Science object lessons are of interest to everyone from age five to ninety-five. Such lessons help our understanding of God's creation and his Word. This book began with three smaller volumes published by Baker Publishing Group under the title *Science and the Bible*. Each volume contained thirty simple object lessons with a Bible application. These earlier lessons are gathered here with many new ideas and activities for successful teaching.

This book contains seventy-seven Bible- and science-related activities. They have been used successfully with small and large groups, both young and old. With help, children can also perform most of the activities at home. Most people have an interest in science, even if they are somewhat intimidated by it. The creation in all its wonder calls out to our hearts and minds for attention. In these activities science ideas are used to illustrate biblical truth. The Lord Jesus freely used everyday objects to communicate his message, including rocks, water, sheep, and flowers.

One major danger with science activities is that they may be remembered while the Scripture lesson is lost. The goal of the presenter should be to reverse this common problem. The activity should be like a compass that points back to the Scripture challenge. When a similar object is seen by the listener weeks or even years later, it can again bring to mind the application of the related Bible lesson. For this reason, all the objects used in these activities are familiar and readily available. Each lesson is divided into three parts: a short Bible lesson, an activity, and a science explanation. The latter is provided for those who want further background information and can be integrated in the actual presentation. Deletions and additions are also encouraged. The lessons are purposely not written for word-by-word repetition. Any effective lesson must be adapted to the presenter's own style.

No effort is made in the lessons to cover every possible aspect of the Christian life. Instead, these particular lessons are chosen to be of practical help for all ages. Every lesson can be made evangelistic with a proper introduction and ending challenge. The lessons include the Old and New Testaments. The New King James Version of Scripture is quoted for the most part.

If you have questions or comments about these activities, feel free to contact the author in care of Baker Publishing Group. It is my hope that this book will encourage the study and enjoyment of the Bible for all ages and that it will stimulate an awareness of the everyday details in God's creation that illustrate biblical truth.

## Ten Hints for Successful Science Object Lessons

1. Don't let activities "steal the show." Start with a presentation of the Scripture. Memorize it if possible. Emphasize the main point of the lesson at the conclusion so the audience will clearly remember it.

2. Practice the science activity ahead of time. Repetition helps bring a smooth delivery, and practice avoids surprises when you are in front of the group. Remember the five P's for object lessons: prior practice prevents poor presentations!

3. Double-check that all needed materials are present and arranged in convenient order. Small details add up to a confident and effective presentation.

4. Adapt activities and Bible lessons to your own situation and interests. Improvise with available materials; insert new ideas of local or current interest. Creativity will hold the attention of your listeners.

5. When unexpected results occur in an activity, laugh and build them into your presentation. The audience will understand and be on your side.

6. Read the background of the Scripture passages. If you are comfortable and familiar with the Bible story, your confidence will be apparent.

7. Good activities use everyday materials. When seen again months later, these items can trigger memory of the Bible lesson. Use of common items may also encourage the audience to try the activities for themselves, extending the learning process.

8. Many of the best activities involve a dramatic point: an unexpected result such as a popping balloon, or something that causes the audience to "ooh and aah." Science activities should be alive and exciting.

9. Have the audience participate as much as possible. Instead of the lecture approach, help the listener be a part of the Scripture lesson and activity.

10. Safety for you and the audience is the highest priority in any science activity. Plan ahead for possible problems; don't take chances. Know where a first aid kit is located. If the activity involves a flame, have a fire extinguisher nearby.

# How Large Is the Sun?

**Theme:** The sun displays God's majesty.

**Bible Verse:** Then God made two great lights: the greater light to rule the day, and the lesser light to rule the night. He made the stars also. (Genesis 1:16)

**Materials Needed:**
- Ruler with millimeter markings
- Calculator
- Paper clip or straight pin
- Several index cards

## Bible Lesson

The creation week was filled with miracle upon miracle as God formed the physical universe. On the fourth day the sun, moon, and stars were set in place. At this time the heavens were filled with a great variety of light sources. The last part of Genesis 1:16 is especially majestic, "He made the stars also." These stars now are known to number in the billions of trillions. In fact, they comprise more than 99.9 percent of the physical creation. The average nighttime star is as large and bright as the sun. In other words, the sun itself is a star. It dominates our sky and our lives simply because it is much closer to us than the many remote evening stars.

Consider the energy available in our sun. Solar energy is thought to be produced by nuclear fusion reactions. The result is continuous nuclear energy production on a scale vastly greater than all of the power plants on earth combined. In fact, every second the sun gives off much more energy than mankind has produced since the beginning of time. And the sun never stops shining; it is always sunrise somewhere on the earth. We benefit from this solar energy in the form of our pleasant morning light. The sun itself is not running out of energy in any perceptible way; its fuel gauge is still on "full." The significance of Genesis 1:16 is clear: God has infinite amounts of energy available to himself, and he also placed unimaginable amounts in the sun and the stars. God is worthy of all our praise.

## Science Activity

Participants will measure the actual size of the sun in a simple way. This activity must be done during the day and at a time when clouds do not hide the sun. First, a pinhole is punched in the center of an index card. This small hole can be made with a paper clip, pin, or pencil point. On a second index card, draw a small circle with a diameter of 2 millimeters, using a ruler and a pen or thin pencil. The circle should be near the center of the card and can be drawn freehand.

Now the punched card is held above the second card as shown in the illustration. Orient the cards in the direction of the sunlight, either while standing outdoors or inside near a window in the path of the sun's rays. A small round image of the sun should appear on the lower card. The pinhole in the upper card acts somewhat like a lens to focus the sunlight. Now adjust the distance between the two cards until the sun's image is roughly the same size as the 2-mm circle drawn on the lower card. While one person holds the cards steady, a second person then measures the cards' separation, also in millimeters. Precision is not needed; let's give this card separation distance the symbol x.

The actual diameter D of the sun can now be found by substituting the measured value of x into this formula,

$$D = \frac{186{,}000{,}000 \text{ miles}}{x}$$

If the x distance is in millimeters, the final answer for the sun's diameter D will be in miles. As a check on the answer, the accurate values are

$$x = 215 \text{ mm (about 8.5 in.)}$$
$$D = 864{,}000 \text{ miles (or 1.4 million km)}$$

Participants will usually get a sun diameter within 10 to 20 percent of the correct value. Differences are mainly due to the difficulty in accurately producing the 2-mm image of the sun on the lower card.

Emphasize the participants' accomplishment: they have measured the vast size of the sun using only a simple ruler! It may be worthwhile to show participants the origin of the formula used. It comes from the similar triangles shown in the figure. The large solar diameter, 864,000 miles, also is typical for many of the nighttime stars. This is a greater distance than many people travel in their entire lifetime. The creation is beyond our understanding, and truly it declares God's great glory and also his great love for us.

## Science Explanation

The formula used to calculate the sun's diameter comes from a proportion based on similar triangles. From the figure,

$$\frac{\text{Sun diameter D}}{\text{Image diameter d}} = \frac{\text{Sun-earth distance X}}{\text{Card separation x}}$$

Solving for D,

$$D = \frac{d\,X}{x}$$

The sun-earth separation X averages 93,000,000 miles. If the image size d is adjusted to 2 millimeters, then

$$D = \frac{2 \text{ mm } (93{,}000{,}000 \text{ miles})}{x}$$

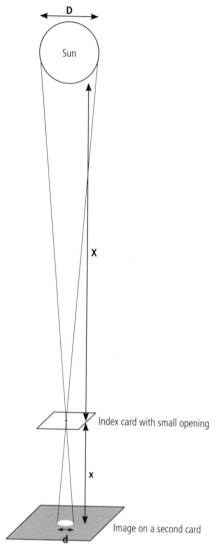

Sunlight passes through a small opening in the upper card, focusing as a small round image on the lower card. Note the narrow triangles with lengths X and x above and below the top card. The drawing is not to scale; the X distance actually is billions of times greater than x.

$$D = \frac{186{,}000{,}000 \text{ miles}}{x}$$

where x is measured in millimeters. Notice that the solar image size does not depend on the size of the pinhole but only on the distance between the cards.

One complicating factor is that the sun is about 2 percent closer to the earth during December and January, and 2 percent farther away during June and July. This variation in distance is due to the earth's elliptical orbit. A slightly smaller sun diameter might therefore be measured in summer when the sun is more distant from earth, and a slightly larger diameter in winter when the sun is closer. This earth-sun distance variation has little effect on our weather. It is the earth's tilt that causes our seasons, not the small change in earth-sun distance.

The pinhole measurement technique also can be used in the evening to measure the diameter of a bright full moon. The equation for moon diameter D with a 2-mm image is

$$D = \frac{477{,}000 \text{ miles}}{x}$$

The moon's actual diameter is 2,160 miles (3,456 kilometers). For this correct answer, the card separation x is 221 millimeters, or about 8.7 inches. Our moon is about 4 times smaller than the earth and 400 times smaller than the sun.

# 2

# Inside a Feather

**Theme:** Feathers show God's design.

**Bible Verse:** Then God said, "Let the waters abound with an abundance of living creatures, and let birds fly above the earth across the face of the firmament of the heavens." (Genesis 1:20)

**Materials Needed:**
- Several feathers (often sold in craft stores)
- Water
- Dish soap

## Bible Lesson

This world is filled with the Creator's handiwork, especially seen in living creatures. Our Bible verse describes the first animal life that appeared on earth, including the sea creatures and the birds. They were supernaturally made in great abundance on the fifth day of the creation. These first animals were not primitive ancestors of today's life. Instead, they were made in all of their intricate complexity. In particular, birds show God's careful attention to detail. Flight in nature is a marvel of engineering. The smallest flying insect displays a greater ability to take off, maneuver, and land than even our most advanced military aircraft.

One day in 1948, the Swiss engineer Georges de Mestral was walking his dog in the woods. Arriving back home, he noticed cockleburs caught in the dog's fur coat. These are round seedpods with a prickly surface that readily cling to clothing or animal fur upon contact. Closer inspection showed tiny hooks on the ends of the burrs. From this finding, de Mestral invented the Velcro fastener made of tiny nylon hooks and loops. Velcro has been called one of the great inventions of the past century, but this fastener actually has been around since the creation of cockleburs. Bird feathers show a similar fastener design in the connections of their side vanes. These are explored in our science activity.

What additional useful ideas remain in nature, awaiting discovery? Surely there are many. God planned all the parts of our world, complete with endless applications and benefits for us to discover and utilize.

## Science Activity

This activity works best if a feather can be given to each person or to selected participants. Packages of colored feathers are often sold in the craft departments of stores. Feathers found in the outdoors probably should not be used since they may not be clean. Note that feathers have a solid, waterproof surface. They provide excellent lightweight insulation. Hold a feather up before the audience and show how the side vanes can be pulled completely apart in several places. Listen closely and you may hear the individual parts, called barbules, snap loose with a click. The feather no longer looks smooth but is instead disorganized.

Now comes the interesting part. With your fingers, stroke softly upward on the sides of the feather several times. The barbs should reattach to one another and once again become a smooth surface. The fasteners within the feather consist of many tiny hooks that grasp each other, equivalent to the Velcro fasteners found on shoes and jackets. The unzipping and quick repair of a feather can be repeated almost endlessly. Birds sometimes separate their feathers in a similar way when cleaning or *preening* them. Clearly, the Creator's Velcro is very durable.

Additional activities with feathers are also of interest. A drop of water placed on the feather will form a round bead, showing the feather is entirely waterproof. If a small trace of soap is added to the water drop, however, the surface tension is broken and the water quickly soaks through the feather. It is important for birds to keep their feathers oiled and waterproof.

As an additional activity, hold a feather horizontally and blow gently across the top surface. The feather should tend to pull upward. This *lift* is how birds and airplanes are able to fly. The air movement decreases the air pressure across the top of the feather or aircraft wing, causing the upward thrust.

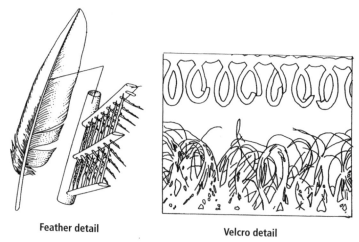

**Feather detail**     **Velcro detail**

Magnified views of a feather and also Velcro. The enlarged feather detail shows the side barbs that connect together. The Velcro has loops that catch and hold nylon strands when the two surfaces are pressed together.

## Science Explanation

A feather's material is made of beta-keratin, a fibrous protein. The figure shows a feather and also a piece of Velcro, each magnified about twenty-five times. The feather's central shaft has side barbs, which in turn have hair-like *barbules*. These are hooked strands that readily grasp each other. Birds also have fluffy *down* feathers that lack the hooks. These small feathers trap air and provide insulation for birds. The cockleburs noticed by Georges de Mestral grow on burdock, a weed that can grow to six feet tall. It successfully scatters its seeds by attaching itself to passing animals.

Some scientists believe that feathers somehow evolved from animal scales over a great span of time. In this view, lizard-like animals such as dinosaurs gradually were transformed into birds. However, the fossil evidence is not convincing. Scales and bird feathers are not at all similar. Each functions uniquely as God intended from the beginning of time.

# Color Codes

**Theme:** The universe is orderly.

**Bible Verse:** Then God blessed them [Adam and Eve], and God said to them, "Be fruitful and multiply; fill the earth and subdue it." (Genesis 1:28)

**Materials Needed:**
- Baking soda
- Red vegetable or fruit juice (cooked red cabbage, beets, cherries, cranberries, unsweetened grape juice, etc.)
- Vinegar

## Bible Lesson

Our selected verse records God's very first commands to mankind. The first is to produce offspring, and the second is to subdue the earth. *Subdue* is a strong word, and it means to manage, understand, and organize the earth. It includes our responsibility to keep the earth's plants, animals, land, water, and air healthy and productive. After all, this world does not belong to us but to the Lord. Psalm 24:1 says, "The earth is the LORD's, and all its fullness." We are therefore called to be stewards, or managers, of God's property.

To care for the earth and utilize its resources successfully, we need to study and understand nature. Many of the great pioneers of modern science were motivated by their confidence that God's world was orderly, predictable, and therefore worthy of inquiry. They saw scientific study as their responsibility, based on Genesis 1:28.

Some Bible critics have suggested that our verse leads directly to environmental abuse and ruin. They claim that the word *subdue* implies an irresponsible license to trash, litter, or ruin the earth. But these critics are entirely wrong. Instead of abuse, Genesis 1:28 commands us to help the earth prosper so that it may continue to display God's glory and artistry.

## Science Activity

The earth's basic materials can be placed into useful categories. These include many liquid chemicals that can be classified as either acids or bases. The acids contain hydrogen and are able to neutralize bases. The bases often feel slippery or soapy; they react with acids to form salts. In the laboratory, various indicators or electronic instruments are used to test liquids to determine their acid or base nature. Many natural indicators are also available. One of the best is the juice from beets or cooked red cabbage. These may not be popular food products, but they are useful in chemistry!

Pour off some of the red juice from a can of beets or cooked red cabbage into a small glass. This juice is a weak acid. Now add about ¼ tablespoon of baking soda and stir. The juice color should turn blue or green, which means that the solution now has become basic in nature. A deeper green color indicates a stronger base. If about ½ tablespoon of vinegar is now added, the solution should return to its red color, back to an acid nature. Pickle juice can also be used since it contains vinegar.

Many other natural juices also change color when combined with acids and bases. These include those mentioned under the *materials needed* section, as well as juice from blueberries, hollyhock plants, rhubarb, and carrot stems. As a science project, you might try testing other colored juices from fruits and vegetables to see how they react with acids and bases. Antacid tablets can also be tested. They are bases that neutralize acids in the stomach.

This activity explores the behavior of acids and bases. The understanding of chemistry is just one part of subduing or understanding the earth and its resources.

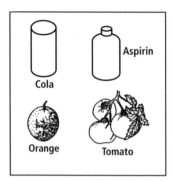

Common acids include vinegar, citrus juices, sauerkraut, and soft drinks. Bases include baking soda, soap, bleach, cleaning supplies, and milk of magnesia.

## Science Explanation

The strength of acids and bases is measured by the level of activity of their hydrogen ions. This is described by their pH number, a chemical symbol that stands for the *power of hydrogen*. Values of pH range from 0 to 14. Acidity is indicated by numbers less than 7. Basic materials, also called *alkalines*, have a pH greater than 8. Neutral materials such as pure water have a pH value of 7 and are neither acidic nor basic. The table lists some pH values for common materials. A change of 1 in pH value represents a tenfold increase in acidic or basic nature.

Many vegetable and fruit color pigments function as acid-base indicators. The common litmus paper used in chemistry labs is extracted from a lichen plant that grows mainly in the Netherlands. The -*mus* in *litmus* has the same origin as the word *moss*.

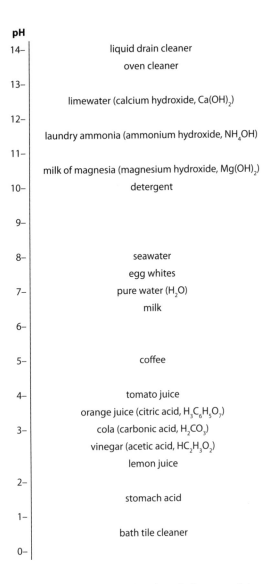

**pH**

| pH | |
|---|---|
| 14– | liquid drain cleaner |
| | oven cleaner |
| 13– | |
| | limewater (calcium hydroxide, $Ca(OH)_2$) |
| 12– | |
| | laundry ammonia (ammonium hydroxide, $NH_4OH$) |
| 11– | |
| | milk of magnesia (magnesium hydroxide, $Mg(OH)_2$) |
| 10– | detergent |
| 9– | |
| 8– | seawater |
| | egg whites |
| 7– | pure water ($H_2O$) |
| | milk |
| 6– | |
| 5– | coffee |
| 4– | tomato juice |
| | orange juice (citric acid, $H_3C_6H_5O_7$) |
| 3– | cola (carbonic acid, $H_2CO_3$) |
| | vinegar (acetic acid, $HC_2H_3O_2$) |
| | lemon juice |
| 2– | |
| | stomach acid |
| 1– | |
| | bath tile cleaner |
| 0– | |

These are pH values for various common liquids, including several chemical formulas. Materials at both ends of the list are very strong, requiring special care in handling.

# Counting Calories

**Theme:** God's laws are dependable.

**Bible Verse:** Thus the heavens and the earth, and all the host of them, were finished. (Genesis 2:1)

**Materials Needed:**
- Quart-sized container
- Ice cubes
- Salt (water softener crystals or table salt)
- Thermometer
- Water

## Bible Lesson

During the creation week God organized matter and energy in the universe. Light appeared across the heavens, and also a great variety of life was formed upon the earth. Many scientific theories have attempted to explain the origin of the universe. Some of these modern ideas are variously called the steady state, big bang, plasma, and quantum fluctuation theories. However, they all fail to adequately explain the beginning of the universe. We simply cannot understand the creation process, because it was supernatural from start to finish. By definition, creation lies beyond our limited, earthly understanding.

The most basic finding in all of nature is called the law of conservation of energy, or the First Law of Thermodynamics. This rule states that energy can be neither created nor destroyed in any process. Energy itself can assume many forms, including chemical, heat, nuclear, light, motion, and sound. However, in every process or experiment all of the involved energy can be exactly accounted for. Not a single new calorie of energy ever appears in nature, nor does an existing calorie disappear. This fundamental law of energy conservation makes the universe a dependable place in which to live. Without this law we could have no confidence in tomorrow's sunshine or even the adequacy of our next breath. Energy conservation probably was established at the end of the creation week when everything was completed and described as "very good." At this time God ceased inserting physical energy into the universe from his infinite reserves.

Science cannot explain the origin of basic physical laws such as the conservation of energy. People seeking a complete understanding of nature must recognize God's provision of the faithful laws that operate the universe. The Creator clearly has a close connection with each physical detail, including energy.

## Science Activity

This small-group activity shows that energy is constant and always accounted for. It involves the production of a low temperature without refrigeration. You might recognize the procedure as the popular way to make homemade ice cream. For ice cream, of course, additional recipe materials are needed.

A quart container is half filled with ice chips. It will help if large ice cubes are crushed to a smaller size. Snow from outdoors can also be used instead of ice if available. Next, add a handful of salt and enough water to make a slush mixture. Stir the mixture, perhaps with a thermometer, and continue to add additional ice and salt as needed.

Keep the thermometer inserted into the brine mixture. You should notice a rapid drop in temperature, well below the normal freezing point of water (32°F, 0°C). If several teams are doing the experiment, they can compete for the lowest temperature attained. Soon the outside of the container will become frosted. A subfreezing temperature as low as 5°F (-15°C) may be reached. If you quickly dip your finger into the slush, you will notice its numbing cold.

The low temperature results from the ice that is forced to melt by the presence of salt. As the ice melts, many calories of energy are absorbed as the water molecules separate into their liquid form. These calories are withdrawn from the surrounding brine solution, thus lowering its temperature. This experiment shows the conservation of energy as calories of energy from the surrounding liquid solution are absorbed in the process of melting the ice.

A mixture of ice, salt, and water results in a very cold temperature.

## Science Explanation

The calorie is one of several possible units for measuring heat energy. One calorie will raise one gram of water by one degree Celsius. A diet calorie, more familiar to us, equals 1,000 of these small water calories. Several other units for measuring energy besides heat include metric joules, British thermal units, kilowatt-hours, and foot-pounds.

To melt one gram of ice requires about eighty calories of heat energy. This quantity is called the latent *heat of fusion* for ice. In the ice-salt mixture the ice is forced to melt by the presence of the salt. To accomplish this, the ice must withdraw calories from the surrounding brine solution. Theoretically, a minimum temperature of -6°F (-21°C) can be reached with an ice and salt mixture if one uses an insulated container. Below this temperature, the ice will coexist with a saturated sodium chloride solution without further melting. This also means that at temperatures below about -6°F, it does little good to put salt on winter highways. Calcium chloride, another chemical spread on winter roads, will continue to melt ice down to -40°F (-40°C).

The study of the behavior of materials at very low temperatures is called *cryogenics*. Many new features of creation are revealed as temperatures fall. These include superconductivity, ultra strong magnetism, and liquefied gases. The lowest possible temperature is called *absolute zero*, -460°F (-273°C). It results when *all* the calories are removed from a sample and atomic motion practically ceases. In cryogenics experiments it is possible to get very close to absolute zero, but it cannot be reached completely. Much of outer space has a low temperature close to absolute zero.

# Pleasant to the Sight

**Theme:** Creation is to be enjoyed.

**Bible Verse:** And out of the ground the LORD God made every tree grow that is pleasant to the sight and good for food. (Genesis 2:9)

**Materials Needed:**
- Old newspapers
- Scissors
- Rubber bands

## Bible Lesson

Trees and other vegetation supernaturally appeared on the earth during the third day of creation. The sun was not made until the next day, but God nevertheless cared for his newly formed plants and trees. As far as we know, the earth is the only place in the universe where plants grow. There is no convincing evidence of life occurring anywhere else, whether on the moon, Mars, or any distant planets.

Trees were given to us by God to serve many useful purposes. Ask the audience for reasons why God made trees. There are many reasons, including the following:

Food such as apple pie and maple syrup

Building materials and furniture

Many products such as paper and rubber

Shade and shelter for animals and people

Medicines derived from trees and plants

Erosion prevention from wind and water

Climbing (a child's suggestion!)

On a more technical note, trees help maintain the health of our atmosphere. All types of vegetation produce oxygen for us to breathe while they absorb carbon dioxide from the air. Vegetation also evaporates or *transpires* moisture into the atmosphere, humidifying the air. A single tree may move hundreds of gallons of water into the air during each growing season.

There is an additional purpose of trees that hasn't yet been mentioned. Our key verse states that trees were made to be pleasant for us to look at. Whether in summer or winter, there is a beauty and majesty to be seen in trees. God created the earth to be a home for us and also to be a delight before our eyes. We should praise God for his artwork that appears all around us, including the trees.

A camping trip or hike in the woods can be very refreshing. One obvious reason is that we are then surrounded by God's creation. For a short time the daily complications of life are put aside, including its interruptions. Many of us make important life decisions while in such an outdoor setting. In this technological age, we need to occasionally refresh our lives by gazing upon the trees and other details of nature that God makes available to us.

## Science Activity

Since paper can be made from trees, this activity humorously reverses the process and attempts to remake a tree from paper. Begin by rolling fifteen to twenty sheets of newspaper together. Each piece should be half of a newspaper page, about 14 inches by 23 inches. Newspaper sheets can easily be torn in half at their crease to make this size. Overlap each newspaper piece by several inches as it is placed on the roll. Wrap the sheets somewhat loosely. When completed, the roll can be held together with rubber bands. Now from one end cut half of the way through the roll in several places with scissors. This is a bit difficult if a greater number of sheets are rolled up; try cutting a few sheets at a time. These cuts will provide the tree branches.

With a large group it is recommended that the roll be almost completed and also cut ahead of time. Then simply add the last couple of sheets and make some final cuts to show the technique during the activity. Now announce that you are about to make a tree. Pull slowly upward on the innermost sheets of the roll. The paper should easily pull upward to an impressive height, at least 4 to 6 feet tall. The scissors cuts will allow the "branches" to spread out and droop downward on all sides. The audience will laugh at the silly appearance of your paper tree, which looks nothing like an outdoor tree, and that is the idea. It is impossible, of course, for anyone to make a real tree. Only God can make a living, beautiful tree.

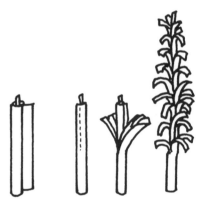

An artificial tree can be made from rolled-up newspaper pages.

## Science Explanation

Our word *paper* comes from *papyrus*, a tall plant that ancient Egyptians pressed, dried, and wrote on. Actual papermaking has been traced to Asia nearly two thousand years ago. In recent centuries, wood pulp replaced rags as the principal source of paper fiber. It was noticed that wasps made paper-like nests by digesting tree and plant material. French scientist Rene Antoine Reaumur described this natural paper production in 1719:

The American wasps form very fine paper. . . . They teach us that paper can be made from the fibers of plants without the use of rags or linens, and seem to invite us to try whether we cannot make fine and good paper from the use of certain woods.

Paper is just one of the many benefits that result from studying the details of creation. Over the centuries, the process of papermaking has remained essentially unchanged. First, wood fibers are separated and wetted to make paper pulp, or stock. This pulp is thinly spread out and compacted to remove water. Binding materials, fillers, and colors may also be added. Many different grades of paper result from these preparation techniques.

The tallest living things on earth are the redwood trees of California, some growing to heights of over 360 feet. Trees are also the oldest living organisms on earth. Some of the living bristlecone pine trees of the western United States are about 4,500 years old. Trees truly are a magnificent part of God's creation and a pleasure to gaze upon.

# Jumping Particles

**Theme:** Music is a gift from God.

**Bible Verse:** His brother's name was Jubal. He was the father of all those who play the harp and flute. (Genesis 4:21)

**Materials Needed:**
- Pen or pencil
- Wide rubber band
- Sand or salt grains
- Sheet of dark cardboard

## Bible Lesson

It is often assumed that people in early times were primitive and uncivilized. Often they are drawn as ape-like or animal-like in appearance. However, the Bible gives a far different picture. From the time of creation, mankind has been given outstanding abilities in thinking and creativity. Tubal-Cain, just six generations from Adam, was a skilled worker of metals (Genesis 4:22). His brother Jubal was a musician who probably designed the instruments that he played. Ever since Jubal, gifted people have had the ability to compose and produce music. The actual instruments mentioned in Genesis 4:21, the harp and flute, are not identified with certainty. The early harp was handheld, and the flute or pipe may have been somewhat like an oboe. Music clearly has been with us since the creation, adding enjoyment to all of our lives. Music is a special gift from God.

## Science Activity

In general, sound may be defined as a vibration. The vibrating objects may be violin strings, a clarinet reed, or your own vocal cords. Our activity makes visible the vibration of small particles. The effect was first seen by scientist Ernst Chladni (1756–1827) two centuries ago.

Lay the stiff, dark cardboard on a table or desk. Hold it in place on the table with a heavy object, and let it extend several inches over the edge. Sprinkle grains of sand, sugar, or salt on the cardboard surface. The grains can now be made to vibrate in interesting ways. Chladni originally stroked the edge of the paper with a violin bow. We can create a similar tool by stretching a wide rubber band along the length of a pen or pencil. Then stroke the cardboard lightly and repeatedly with the rubber band in a downward direction. This takes some practice, but the cardboard should soon begin to vibrate at various points on its surface. Notice how the grains "dance" up and down on the cardboard surface at the locations of maximum vibration. Elsewhere, in quiet areas, the grains will accumulate. The vibration moves from the rubber band to the cardboard, then to the particles themselves. Invisible air molecules likewise vibrate, carrying sound to your ear.

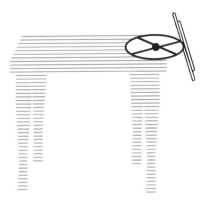

A drawing of Chladni's original experiment. Several of his sand figures are shown also. When a square plate vibrates, sand grains accumulate in the darker areas.

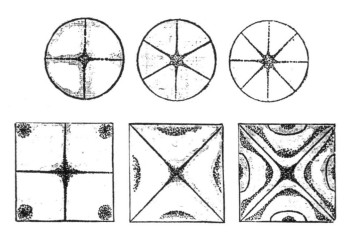

Typical sand patterns obtained on round and square surfaces.

## Science Explanation

Chladni carried out a series of experiments on various shapes of thin metal plates. He observed many complex vibration patterns using sand grains. In this way he was able to explain the different ways that a drum vibrates. Some of his patterns are shown in the figure. Surface areas that vibrate vigorously are called *antinodes*. The quiet regions, lying between the vibrating portions, are called *nodes*. At nodes the grains settle and lie relatively still. It is found that when one portion of a plate moves slightly upward, the adjacent portion moves downward. Thus, adjacent areas vibrate oppositely. Drumheads likewise can be made to vibrate in many different symmetric patterns, depending on how they are struck. Each pattern produces a slightly different sound. It was Chladni who first made these drum vibrations visible. The wooden surfaces of guitars and violins have similar vibration patterns. The sand patterns in the figure show the symmetry and beauty of vibrations. Sound is a remarkable gift from God.

# There Go the Continents

**Theme:** The Genesis flood was worldwide.

**Bible Verse:** In the six hundredth year of Noah's life, in the second month, the seventeenth day of the month, on that day all the fountains of the great deep were broken up, and the windows of heaven were opened. (Genesis 7:11)

**Materials Needed:**
- Enlarged copies of the map provided
- Scissors

## Bible Lesson

The world today is very different from the original creation. This lesson suggests that the continents and the seas themselves were completely reshaped at the time of the great flood of Noah's day. Genesis 7:11 describes the bursting forth of the "springs" or "fountains" of the great deep. This verse describes a worldwide fracturing of the earth's crust. Subterranean water then moved upward from ground reservoirs as the rain fell. The world's climate also changed after the flood, from uniformly mild to our current seasonal changes. These physical effects show the global extent of the Genesis flood.

Many scientists reject the idea of a worldwide flood, and they thereby miss a key event in earth history. Many modern theologians also deny the flood story. As a result, they miss the vital message that while God is patient with the sin of mankind, global judgment comes eventually. And when judgment comes, it is complete. In Noah's day, water was used to cleanse the earth. According to 2 Peter 3:12, fire will purify the earth in a future day. This is surely a fearful thought to those who do not acknowledge their Creator. For believers, however, it is an encouragement to realize that someday all things will be made right and faithfulness will be rewarded.

## Science Activity

Enlarged copies should be made of the map figure ahead of time. It shows the continents and also the locations of many earthquakes. Quakes tend to occur along lines where the earth's crust is fractured, or faulted. Participants are asked to cut out some of the continents and fit them together like puzzle pieces. It is preferable if no instruction is given on which continents fit where. Most participants will quickly "discover" the South America–Africa fit. Connections between

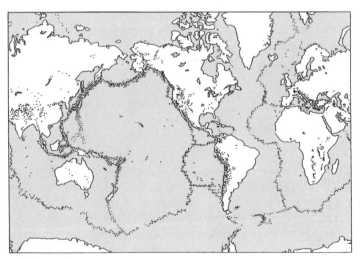

From the National Oceanic and Atmospheric Administration (NOAA).

A map of the world. The dots are the locations of earthquakes, called *epicenters*. They occur along fractures and weak regions of the earth's crust.

other land areas are less obvious due to coastal erosion and complex motions of the continents.

Participants may also notice that South America and Africa fit snugly against the fault line in the middle of the Atlantic Ocean. It is helpful if a second copy of the map is available on which to place the cut-out "puzzle pieces." During the flood event the earth's land surface was broken up into the continents we observe today. Continental drift, also called seafloor spreading, thus fits into biblical history. It began dramatically and rapidly with the Genesis flood and still continues today at a much slower pace.

## Science Explanation

In 1912, scientist Alfred Wegener first suggested that the earth's continents had split up and drifted apart. His idea was scoffed at and rejected by others for several decades. Today, however, geologists recognize the existence of an original "supercontinent" called *Pangaea*. They believe that about 200 million years ago, Pangaea broke up gradually into the separate continents of today.

In the creation view presented here, the great flood triggered the original Pangaea breakup. The continents were rapidly driven apart due to the worldwide geologic disturbance. The Mid-Atlantic ridge or fault line, shown on the map, remains as one of many great scars from this catastrophic breakup event. The ongoing slow drift of the continents is probably a much-diminished "leftover" motion from the original flood event.

The solid outer part of the earth is called the *crust*. It averages 40 miles thick, and it actually floats on the denser mantle of melted rock beneath. The density of the crust averages 3 $g/cm^3$, while the mantle density is greater, around 3.5 to 5.5 $g/cm^3$. The crust is divided into several large plates, similar to puzzle pieces. Some of the edges of these plates are *ridges*, where new crustal material is moving upward and outward from below. The Mid-Atlantic ridge is one example. Other plate edges are called *trenches*, where the crust is bending down into the mantle and remelting. This occurs near Indonesia, a region of severe earthquake activity. The continents are carried along as the plates slowly move horizontally, somewhat like conveyor belts. Another illustration of the earth's dynamic crust is the surface of a pot of heated soup. Heat convection causes heated soup to move to the top, then spread outward to the sides of the pot, then downward again. Likewise, new crust material moves upward from the mantle to the earth's surface, then outward.

Satellites measure the exact positions of North America, Europe, and South America, and find them to be moving apart at a rate of 0.5 to 2 inches per year. At the time of the great flood, when continental breakup first occurred, the motion could have been greatly accelerated.

# Watch for the Rainbow

**Theme:** The rainbow is a reminder that God's promises do not fail.

**Bible Verse:** I set My rainbow in the cloud, and it shall be for the sign of the covenant between Me and the earth. (Genesis 9:13)

**Materials Needed:**
- One or more CD or DVD discs
- Sunshine, desk light, or flashlight

## Bible Lesson

God placed a rainbow in the clouds at the end of the great flood in Noah's day. This was a visible sign of God's promise that there would never be another worldwide flood. This was a covenant, a firm agreement or promise between two parties. In this case, God reached out to the future generations of Noah and all living creatures and declared his love. Ever since the flood, local rainstorms have often been followed by beautiful rainbows. God remembers this rainbow promise after thousands of years, just as he faithfully keeps all the promises of his Word. Other favorite Scripture promises may be given or requested from participants to enhance the lesson.

## Science Activity

A rainbow appears when sunlight is dispersed into its many component colors by water droplets in the sky. These rainbow colors always have the same order: red, orange, yellow, green, blue, indigo, violet. "Roy G. Biv" is a useful mnemonic for the order of colors. When rays of colored light overlap, the familiar white light appears.

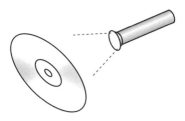

White light divides into bright colors when it reflects from a CD or DVD disc.

Most of us have seen a rainbow form in the spray from a fountain or water hose on a sunny day. When indoors, a rainbow is more challenging to produce and requires semidarkness. For this lesson we can produce some of the rainbow colors, either inside or outside, using a CD or DVD. Experiment ahead of time with sunlight, a lamp, or a flashlight directed at the shiny side of the disc. When looking at the disc at various angles, the rainbow colors are readily noticed. If several discs are available to participants, use "extras" since discs scratch easily. Used discs often can be found at secondhand stores.

## Science Explanation

CDs and DVDs are covered with many small, circular grooves. When playing a disc, a laser beam moves along the grooves and is deflected by microscopic bumps. This signal is then converted into sound or pictures by electronics. When a light beam reflects from the disc surface, certain colors are enhanced and others are diminished in a process called light interference. White light is similarly separated into its component colors by butterfly wings, an oil film on water, seashells, and soap bubbles.

Light is a complex subject, still not fully understood by scientists. The words "God is light" (1 John 1:5) remind us of his divine nature and attributes. Light is a fitting picture of our Creator because both are beautiful, pure, and the opposite of darkness.

# A Large Number

**Theme:** God's family is large and growing.

**Bible Verse:** I will multiply your [Abraham's] descendants as the stars of the heaven and as the sand which is on the seashore. (Genesis 22:17)

**Materials Needed:**
- Small amount of sand
- Magnifying glasses (optional)
- Small rulers

## Bible Lesson

In Genesis 22, Abraham's obedience was tested regarding the sacrifice of his son Isaac. Abraham was willing to obey, and God provided a ram instead. Then God promised Abraham a great family blessing. Abraham's descendants would number as many as the stars in the sky and the sand grains on the seashore. Today, four thousand years later, all believers can be called the "children of Abraham." True to Scripture, no one knows the total number of Christians worldwide and throughout the ages, surely numbering in the billions. God's kingdom is still growing, even in this troubled world, as people acknowledge their Creator and call upon his name.

## Science Activity

Sand grains provide a good example of an extremely large number. Participants are challenged to count some individual sand grains, and then to estimate the total grains on all the seashores of the world. There is some math involved, but the exercise is worth the effort.

Give each participant a ruler and a pinch of sand. If sand is not available, salt or sugar can also be used. The particles can be sprinkled on a dark smooth surface that shows them clearly. The goal is to count the number of grains along a 1-inch length of ruler. With the ruler edge, push some of the grains into a line and begin counting. The exact number is not necessary and depends on the particle size. A magnifier may be helpful. My own 1-inch lineup totaled nearly 100 sand grains.

Now we need to estimate the number of sand grains in a cubic inch, or handful of sand. Take the lineup number and multiply it times itself twice, cubing it. If the initial number was 100, then $100^3$ is 1,000,000 or $10^6$. Going further, a fair estimate for the sand on all the seashores of the world is $10^{16}$ cubic inches, or 10 thousand trillion cubic inches. (See the science explanation for the origin of this number.) Multiplying these two numbers gives the worldwide total of sand grains:

$$10^6 \times 10^{16} = 10^{22}$$

The final number obtained by participants should be close to this result. This number estimates all the sand grains on the earth's shorelines. Amazingly, it is also approximately the total number of *known* stars in the universe. In words, this number equals 10 billion trillion stars or sand grains. Such a vast number is beyond our comprehension. The meaning of Genesis 22:17 is not that Abraham will have exactly $10^{22}$ offspring. Instead, the promise is that God's family is beyond counting, and it's still growing!

## Science Explanation

Most sand grains consist of quartz fragments made of silicon dioxide, $SiO_2$. This common mineral has a high hardness and is not easily dissolved or chemically altered. As a result it lies on many beaches in abundance as an end product of rock erosion.

Sand grains are lined up along the edge of a ruler and counted.

Let's estimate the number of cubic inches of sand on all the earth's seashores ($10^{16}$), as used in the science activity. As a rough guess, assume there is a total of a million miles of sandy seashores. This number equals 42 trips around the earth and includes the many irregular shorelines. Further, assume the average beach is 100 feet wide and filled to a depth of 10 feet with sand. These would seem to be a conservative estimate. Now convert all three numbers to inches—length, width, and depth—and multiply them to get the total sand volume in cubic inches. There are 63,360 inches in one mile. The final answer is close to $10^{16}$ cubic inches. As earlier, multiply this number by 1 million to obtain the total sand grains, $10^{22}$.

This is also approximately the total number of photographed stars within all the galaxies of the known universe. This is more than a trillion stars for every person on earth. Whether one considers sand grains or stars, both show God's great glory.

# A Stairway to Heaven

**Theme:** We are always in touch with heaven.

**Bible Verse:** Then he [Jacob] dreamed, and behold, a ladder was set up on the earth, and its top reached to heaven; and there the angels of God were ascending and descending on it. (Genesis 28:12)

**Materials Needed:**
- Table or other flat surface
- Rectangular game blocks (e.g., dominoes, Jenga blocks, building blocks, etc.)

## Bible Lesson

Jacob had recently pretended to be his twin brother, Esau, in order to receive his father Isaac's blessing. Esau was very angry about this deception and vowed to kill Jacob. Jacob therefore quickly left home and traveled far to visit his uncle Laban. Along the way, he rested for the evening in the outdoors, using a stone for a pillow.

During the night, God spoke to Jacob in an unusual dream. Jacob saw a stairway or ladder stretched between heaven and earth. Moving up and down this passageway were angels. God also spoke to Jacob in the dream, comforting him. This vision from God is rich in meaning.

The ladder symbolizes Christ, who bridges the gap between heaven and earth (John 1:51). The angels are ministering spirits on earth, active at all times, both day and night. Through prayer and obedience, we thus have access to God in heaven. This is true wherever we are, whether at home or in a wilderness setting like Jacob.

## Science Activity

This activity works best with individuals or with groups of two to three people. A model stairway is built by stacking blocks upward, each one offset from those beneath. Lower blocks are gradually spaced outward, with the top block extending outward half its length as shown in the figure. The goal, perhaps as a contest, is to be the first to have the top block overhang completely from the bottom block. The result is quite impressive to see, especially if the blocks are stacked at the edge of a table, extending outward over open space.

Each participant should have eight or more blocks. Actually, a complete overhang is possible with just four blocks above the base block. Have participants continue to stack the blocks, cantilevered outward. The project is fun and also frustrating when an unfinished

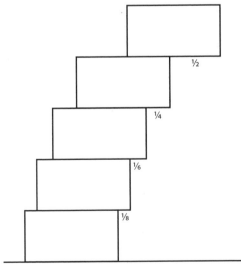

A leaning stairway of blocks, with offsets of ½ (top block), ¼, ⅙, ⅛, etc. No part of the top block is above the bottom block.

stack of blocks collapses. This simple block stairway illustrates Jacob's dream. That remarkable stairway extended upward to heaven and assured Jacob of God's presence during his time of need.

## Science Explanation

A stack of blocks will balance as long as its *center of gravity* or balance point is supported by the table. The Leaning Tower of Pisa in Milan, Italy, likewise stands because its center of gravity lies above the base, even though the structure is tilted to the side.

A stack of blocks is *just* at the point of tipping when the amount of block overlaps, from the top down, are ½, ¼, ⅙, ⅛, etc. In this case, the center of gravity is positioned directly above the outer edge of the bottom block. This arrangement is shown in the figure. The total overhang is then equal to

$$½ + ¼ + ⅙ + ⅛ +$$

Mathematicians call this sum a *harmonic* series. Curiously, even though the terms rapidly decrease, their sum increases slowly with no upper limit as more terms (or blocks) are added. In mathematical words, this harmonic series is said to *diverge*. The following table gives some calculated overhang values for stacked blocks, including some large theoretical numbers.

| Number of blocks | Possible overhang |
| --- | --- |
| 1 | .5 |
| 4 | 1.04 |
| 6 | 1.225 |
| 10 | 1.46 |
| 227 | 3.1 |
| $2.72 \times 10^8$ | 10.1 |

The table shows that an overhang of one whole block is possible with a stack of just four blocks above the base. A tower of 227 blocks, probably an impossible feat, could overhang by three full blocks. Cantilever bridges are likewise built with beams that project outward toward each other, joining to form a span without any need of a center support.

# Plug into God's Power

**Theme:** God's power is available to us if we are willing to reach out for it.

**Bible Verse:** But indeed for this purpose I have raised you up, that I may show My power in you, and that My name may be declared in all the earth. (Exodus 9:16)

**Materials Needed:**
- Several batteries, AAA, AA, C, or D size
- Flashlight bulbs, 3-volt (this is the usual value for small bulbs)
- 6-inch lengths of wire, either insulated or bare

## Bible Lesson

Moses was afraid to lead the Israelites out of Egypt. In Exodus 6:12 and 30, Moses told the Lord that he had faltering lips; he lacked power and confidence. However, the Lord promised to give Moses the words he needed to say. When Moses later stood before Pharaoh, the words of the Lord did indeed flow through him and Aaron. Moses thus became the leader of the entire nation of Israel. The Bible verse quoted above actually refers to the raising up of Pharaoh, whom the Lord also used to reveal his great power (Exodus 9:16).

God's power is still available to us today if we are willing to live for him. We may not rule nations as did Moses or Pharaoh, but our daily walk can be an important testimony and encouragement to others. God's power can also help us live an upright life in an upside-down world. If we call on the name of the Lord Jesus to rule our lives, his power becomes ours. Let us follow Moses in obedience rather than follow Pharaoh in failure. A personal testimony of victory in Christ would be suitable at this point of the lesson.

## Science Activity

This activity is designed for individuals or small groups of two to four. Each person or group is given a battery, a bulb, and a length of wire. If the wire is insulated, both ends should be stripped about a half inch to expose the metal. The challenge is to make the bulb light up by connecting the three items correctly. The electrical energy is available within the battery; the trick is getting it to move through the bulb. Give no help as the teams try various combinations of circuits. In a few minutes, bulbs will begin to light and group members can then show each other how it is done. Of the many possible combinations, only a couple will result in light; most arrangements are unsuccessful.

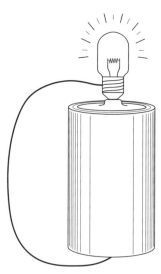

One possible arrangement that will light a flashlight bulb.

One caution: If the wire is connected directly across both ends of the battery and held there for a length of time, the wire may become uncomfortably warm. This is called a short circuit. However, there is no shock hazard in this activity.

## Science Explanation

To light the bulb, a series electrical circuit must be constructed. This requires a complete loop, including both ends of the battery and also both electrical contacts on the light bulb, the side and end. The series circuit provides a complete conducting path for electrons to travel through the bulb.

Electrons are the tiny electrical charges that produce current and power. When the bulb is lit, about 10 million trillion ($10^{19}$) electrons pass through the filament each second. Electricity is part of the truly amazing world of microscopic particles.

# The Crystal Garden

**Theme:** God makes a garden grow.

**Bible Verse:** Now it came to pass on the next day that Moses went into the tabernacle of witness, and behold, the rod of Aaron, of the house of Levi, had sprouted and put forth buds, had produced blossoms and yielded ripe almonds. (Numbers 17:8)

**Materials Needed:**
- Pieces of brick, charcoal, or any porous solid
- Glass bowl or dish
- Small container
- Laundry bluing (usually available in laundry supplies)
- Salt
- Household ammonia
- Food coloring

## Bible Lesson

The Old Testament Israelites went through many cycles of rebellion against God, followed by repentance and restoration. Numbers 16 describes the rebellion of Korah and 250 of his followers. They attempted to declare themselves priests, a privilege reserved for Aaron's family. In judgment they all were swallowed up by an earthquake. To make absolutely clear the special place of the house of Aaron, God led Moses to give an object lesson. A wooden staff or walking stick from each of the twelve tribes of Israel, with the tribe's name inscribed, was placed in the Tent of Testimony. When inspected the next day, the only staff that looked different was Aaron's rod. It had supernaturally sprouted leaves and produced fruit. Here was a real example of "Miracle Grow"! The lesson was clear that Aaron's family was chosen by God to minister to the Israelites.

It is God who causes every plant to grow on the earth; he is the source of all life. At God's command, even a dead staff produces leaves and almonds. The one who controls the laws of nature is able to alter these laws at will, just as he did for Moses. God is all-powerful.

## Science Activity

This project takes several days to perform. In a small container mix 4 tablespoons (T) of bluing, 4 T of water, 2 T of salt, and 1 T of ammonia. Avoid breathing this mixture. Pour the solution over fragments of charcoal or brick in the bowl. Also put drops of food coloring on various parts of the charcoal; then leave the bowl undisturbed for several days.

A crystal garden can be grown with household materials.

Crystals will slowly grow like coral on the hard surfaces over two or three days. They are typically white and the food coloring will give them variety. The crystals are very fragile; notice their intricate, feathery structure. The crystals will eventually collapse and fragments will begin growing throughout the bowl.

## Science Explanation

The brick or charcoal provides a surface on which crystallization can occur. Capillary action causes the solution to soak upward through the fragments. Then, as the water evaporates, the chemical portion of the solution is left behind, forming the flower-like crystals of solid salt. The rate of growth depends on the temperature and humidity of the room. Low humidity will speed the process.

Crystal growth involves much unseen activity on the submicroscopic level. To produce visible crystals in two to three days, hundreds of chemical molecules must move through the charcoal and arrange themselves into the crystal lattice *every second*. The budding staff described in our Bible story is even more complex than crystal growth. Crystals are not alive and certainly cannot produce almonds overnight! The growth of Aaron's staff was a miraculous sign from God.

# Mystery Loops

**Theme:** God tells us what we need to know about life.

**Bible Verse:** The secret things belong to the LORD our God, but those things which are revealed belong to us and to our children forever, that we may do all the words of this law. (Deuteronomy 29:29)

**Materials Needed:**
- Roll of cash register or adding machine tape 2 to 3 inches wide
- Masking tape
- Pens or pencils

## Bible Lesson

On this side of heaven the Christian does not have simple answers to many difficult questions, such as:

How did God create the universe from nothing?

How can God be three persons in one?

Why is there suffering in the world?

Why does Jesus love me?

We cannot expect to completely understand these deep truths. Only God has full understanding, and his ways are past finding out (Romans 11:33). It is like seeing an unclear image in a mirror. The picture is there but the details are blurry. At a future time all the un-solved mysteries of life will be made clear. From the vantage point of heaven, our questions will quickly disappear. This truth should be a comfort to the believer during troubling times. Someday we will better understand God's purpose in events. We will realize how he answered our prayers in the best possible, loving way. Meanwhile, life's mysteries provide opportunities to exercise our faith in God.

## Science Activity

This activity can be done by each person as you demonstrate. The results are fun and unexpected. Begin by giving each person a paper strip about 3 to 4 feet long. If the strips are torn from a roll they will tend to roll up, but this does not matter. Stretch your paper strip out straight, and give one end a half twist (180 degrees). Bring the two ends of the paper strip together and fasten them with a piece of masking tape. This should make a twisted, curled up loop.

Now ask participants to draw a line along the outside of their loop. This can be done freehand; we just want to make a visible mark along the loop with a pencil or pen. The result is surprising: when the line arrives back at its start, the entire strip will be lined. The line appears everywhere. The strange conclusion is that the loop of paper somehow only has one side. Next, make a small tear along the pencil line and continue tearing the entire length of the loop by hand, including directly through the taped connection. When complete, the result should be a single loop that is twice as large as the original loop.

Start over again with new strips of paper, and this time make a full 360-degree twist in one end before taping together to make a loop. As before, tear the strip roughly along the center along its entire length. The result now should be two linked loops, somewhat like a paper chain. There are several other unexpected results possible depending on the number of twists in the original paper strip.

The paper strips have surprising and mysterious properties, and the mathematical description of the results is very complex. We may not understand how the results of the paper twisting work, but they are real nevertheless. Likewise there is much we do not understand about our Maker. Still, the Bible makes clear the gospel invitation of salvation through the Lord Jesus.

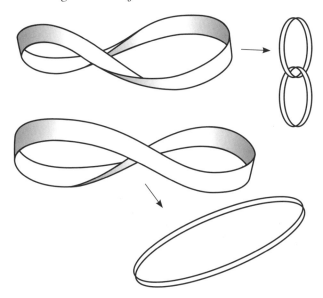

Paper loops with a twist lead to unexpected results.

## Science Explanation

The loops of paper are called Mobius strips, named for August Mobius (Mo'-be-us, 1790–1868). The paper strips involve an advanced branch of mathematics called *topology*. Similar long, single-twist strips of material, with just one side or boundary, find application for conveyor and pulley belts. Such belts last twice as long as untwisted belts before wearing out. The Mobius shape also appears in nature; for example, in the flexible, ribbon-shaped crystalline form of $NbSe_3$ (niobium selenide), an alloy of the metals niobium and selenium. Mobius shapes are also utilized in art and sculpture.

# The Floating Ax Head

**Theme:** God has power over nature.

**Bible Verse:** So the man of God [Elisha] said, "Where did it fall?" And he showed him the place. So he cut off a stick, and threw it in there; and he made the iron float. (2 Kings 6:6)

**Materials Needed:**
- Clear, tall glass jar or bud vase
- ½ cup each
  * Dark Karo syrup, molasses, or honey (tan color)
  * Liquid dish soap (blue or green)
  * Vegetable oil (yellow)
  * Rubbing alcohol (clear)
  * Water (any color)
- Several small objects
  * Cork
  * Small candle
  * Penny
  * Large eraser
  * Pencil-tip eraser
  * Raisin
  * Button
- Food coloring

## Bible Lesson

This Old Testament story is of special interest because it is less familiar than many others and is mentioned only once in the Bible. It involves a miracle by which God solved a workman's problem. Certain Israelites had gone to the Jordan River to settle. They were cutting wood for shelters when a minor accident occurred. An ax head came loose, flew through the air, and landed in the river. The workman was distressed over losing a borrowed tool, and he asked for help. Elisha located the spot where the metal piece had sunk and tossed in a stick. Miraculously, the heavy ax head floated to the surface and was retrieved by the workman.

This rarely mentioned miracle shows God's complete power over nature, even in the smallest details. In truth, of course, no miracle is small. Each is a temporary reversal of the fundamental physical laws of nature. This ax head miracle answered the simple plea for help from an unnamed workman. It also encouraged Elisha and the others, and showed God's great glory.

## Science Activity

This activity can be set up ahead of time or done with a small group. It explores liquids and objects of different densities. The idea is to help visualize the floating ax head story.

Slowly pour the liquids one at a time into the glass jar, perhaps over a spoon so they do not mix. The narrower the jar, the better the result will be. Pour the liquids in the order listed—most dense first and least dense last. If one of the ingredients is missing the activity will still work:

Syrup or molasses

Dish soap

Water

Vegetable oil

Rubbing alcohol

When poured gently, the liquids should remain separate in distinct layers. Keep the amounts in proportion to nearly fill the container. Avoid getting the sticky syrup on the sides of the container.

Now introduce several small objects into the mixture. Gently place the objects on the surface and observe them. Certain items will float at a particular layer, while others will sink. Each object seeks its own resting place depending on its own density or heaviness. The final product is an interesting sight with the distinct liquids and suspended objects. For visual effect, add food coloring to the water before pouring it into the jar, and also use small objects that are colorful.

Explain to the group that the iron ax head that floated in water is an entirely different case that cannot be duplicated. Our liquids and objects are obeying scientific laws; the ax head obeyed God's direct command.

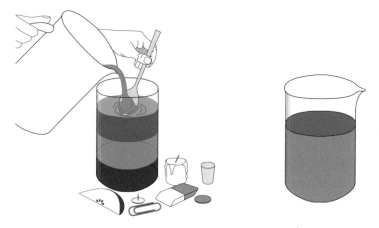

A clear container shows the colorful separation of liquids with different densities.

## Science Explanation

Floating or sinking depends on the densities of materials. Density can be measured in grams per cubic centimeter ($g/cm^3$). Density takes into account an object's weight and also its size. The following table compares densities for several common materials.

| Material | Density ($g/cm^3$) |
|---|---|
| Cork | 0.24 |
| Wood | 0.3–0.6 |
| Rubbing alcohol | 0.87 |

| Material | Density (g/cm³) |
|---|---|
| Vegetable oil | 0.91 |
| Water | 1.0 |
| Dishwashing liquid | 1.03 |
| Syrup | 1.37 |
| Iron ax head | 7.9 |
| Penny | 9.0 |
| Liquid mercury | 13.6 |
| Gold | 19.3 |

Water density is assigned the value of 1.0 by the definition of the gram and cubic centimeter. Objects with density less than 1.0 will float in water; denser objects will sink.

# God's Invisible Power

**Theme:** God surrounds and protects us with unseen power.

**Bible Verse:** And Elisha prayed, and said, "LORD, I pray, open his eyes that he may see." Then the LORD opened the eyes of the young man, and he saw. And behold, the mountain was full of horses and chariots of fire all around Elisha. (2 Kings 6:17; see also 2 Kings 6:16 and Psalm 34:7)

**Materials Needed:**
- Magnet
- Iron filings, paper clips, or staples
- Dish with water
- Scrap of paper towel
- Needle or pin
- Overhead projector (optional)

## Bible Lesson

The Arameans were warring against Israel. The enemy especially wanted to capture Elisha because he knew their military moves ahead of time. When Elisha's servant saw that the enemy had surrounded them, he panicked. Elisha then declared that "those who are with us are more than those who are with them" (2 Kings 6:16). He prayed that the ever-present power of the Lord would be revealed to this servant. Immediately the hills were seen to be filled with horses and chariots of fire. The enemy was ultimately turned aside by blindness (2 Kings 6:18–23).

## Science Activity

There are many things in this world that are real even though we cannot see them. Consider a small, permanent magnet. Completely surrounding this magnet is an invisible magnetic field. Put a sheet of paper over the magnet and sprinkle iron filings, staples, or paper clips on it, showing their alignment. (Do not let fine iron filings touch the magnet as they will be difficult to remove.) This activity also works well on an overhead projector screen, with the magnet placed under a transparency sheet. You can comment that the invisible angelic powers that surround believers are just as real as the invisible magnetic field.

The earth also has magnetism that can be demonstrated. Float a needle in a dish of water by carefully laying the needle on a scrap of floating paper towel. Then sink the paper out from under the needle by pushing downward and soaking it. You may be able to float the needle directly by carefully lowering it into the water.

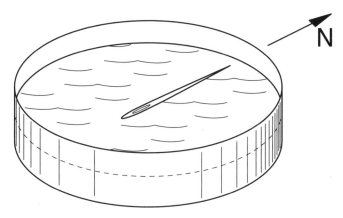

A needle will float on the surface of the water and point north if magnetized.

The needle will float because of the surface tension or "stickiness" of water; it should also orient itself to the north. Most needles and pins are naturally magnetized. (If not already magnetic, stroke the needle or pin a few times against a permanent magnet.) Rotate the needle slightly on the surface of the water and it will again return to the north direction. This works well for larger groups by using an overhead projector and a water dish with a clear bottom. A real compass can also be used to show the earth's magnetism, but this homemade floating compass is more interesting.

Just as the invisible angels protected Elisha and his servant, the earth's magnetic field also keeps us from harm. Radiation constantly flows toward the earth from the sun in what is called the solar wind. This wind of high-speed particles would harm us if the earth's magnetism didn't deflect the particles and prevent them from hitting us. Instead, their path is bent to the far north and south where they harmlessly enter the polar regions of the earth. There they sometimes give a glow to the atmosphere, which causes the aurora, or northern and southern lights.

We are surrounded by a number of invisible shields, including magnetism and the ozone layer. Even greater is the divine protection that the Lord revealed to Elisha and his servant long ago.

## Science Explanation

The surface tension of water allows a needle, a razor blade, or a water bug to float directly on the liquid surface. Surface tension is unusually high for water, compared with most other liquids. Within a water molecule ($H_2O$), a hydrogen atom (H) that is covalently bonded to an oxygen atom (O) is also attracted to surrounding oxygen atoms. The separate water molecules in a sense "hold hands" as they attract each other. This results in the high surface tension or stickiness of water.

Surface tension reveals itself in many ways. It causes the spherical shape of raindrops, fog, and cloud droplets. It also causes fluid to cling to our joints for internal lubrication. In addition, surface tension explains how sap is able to climb upward in trees, as water molecules pull upward on one another. Without water's outstanding cohesiveness, trees could not possibly grow tall. Flowers and plant leaves would also be in trouble. It is the changing water pressure within tiny capillaries that causes leaves to fold by night and also opens blossoms by day. In many ways water is a very special and essential resource.

# An Invisible Army

**Theme:** A host of angels defends the believer.

**Bible Verse:** And Elisha prayed, and said, "Lord, I pray, open his eyes that he may see." Then the Lord opened the eyes of the young man, and he saw. And behold, the mountain was full of horses and chariots of fire all around Elisha. (2 Kings 6:17)

**Materials Needed:**
- Lemon juice or vinegar
- Nails, paper clips, straight pins, or safety pins
- Several pennies
- Shallow glass or dish

## Bible Lesson

Elisha was a faithful prophet who took upon himself the mantle and testimony of Elijah. Elisha experienced many wonderful instances of God's grace. In 2 Kings 6, a conflict is described between Israel and their opponents, the Syrians or Arameans. The Lord continually showed Elisha the plans of the Syrians ahead of time, thus ruining their strategy of attack. This enraged the king of Aram, and he sent his army to capture the prophet Elisha.

Early in the morning, Elisha's servant looked outward from their village and saw the enemy gathered all around them with horses and chariots. He cried to Elisha, "Oh, my lord, what shall we do?" Elisha told his servant, "Don't be afraid." This wonderful phrase of comfort occurs 365 times throughout Scripture. Elisha then prayed that the servant's eyes could see the Lord's protecting army. Immediately the servant saw the hills full of horses and chariots of fire. He then realized the truth of Elisha's words, "Those who are with us are more than those who are with them" (v. 16; see also Psalm 68:17). No battle followed because the enemy was struck with temporary blindness. Instead, Elisha showed mercy to the army that had opposed Israel.

## Science Activity

Just as the spirit world cannot be seen, individual atoms of matter are also invisible. This activity involves the motion of copper atoms, which can only be seen after many millions of them accumulate. Place several pennies in a shallow glass or dish. Add enough vinegar or lemon juice to cover the coins, and add a pinch of salt. Since vinegar and lemon juice are weak acids, copper atoms will begin to dissolve from the pennies.

Now other metal items are needed for the copper coating process. Paper clips, pins, or nails work well. These items need to be cleaned first, ideally with soap and water. A clean metal surface is important. The objects are then placed in the penny-acid solution; they can lay directly on the pennies.

After thirty minutes, withdraw the metal objects. A slight copper-colored coating should be visible on them. This copper layer is bonded to the metal and should not rub off. If left in the solution for several hours, the metal objects should take on a shiny copper appearance. If bubbles appear on the coins or objects, they can be shaken off.

During this plating process, millions of copper atoms actually accumulate on the metal objects each second. There is a vast crowd of unseen copper atoms moving between the pennies and the metal. Yet the copper atoms are so plentiful that no loss is noticeable from the pennies. One is reminded of the unseen host of angels that protected Elisha in the Old Testament story. The copper-coated objects can be kept by participants as a reminder of the lesson.

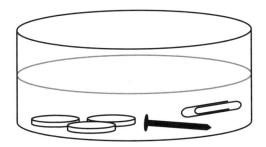

A paper clip, pin, or nail can be copper plated with pennies in a weak acid solution.

## Science Explanation

The number of copper atoms involved in the plating process is truly astounding. Suppose that the completed copper layer on the metal becomes visible at just 0.01 millimeters thick, or 0.0004 inches. This is ten times less than the thickness of a sheet of paper, yet represents a thickness of about 1 million atoms. If this thin layer accumulates in one hour, then a thickness of nearly 300 new copper atoms must attach to the nail each second. In other words, there is a mighty rush of copper atoms through the solution and to the nail, each atom fitting into a regular crystal structure on the metal surface.

Pennies made before 1982 are mostly copper with some zinc added. From 1982 onward, pennies are made of zinc with only a thin copper coating. The year of the coin does not matter in this exercise, though, since even the newer coated pennies have sufficient copper.

There are several different techniques for the commercial plating process. These include electroplating, anodizing, and chemical plating. Plating with electricity gives more effective results, but the chemical method described here is simpler. Lemon juice is a diluted form of citric acid, $C_6H_8O_7H_2O$. Vinegar is acetic acid, $CH_3OOH$. These acids dissolve the surface copper atoms from the pennies. With a vast number of copper atoms in solution, some find their way to the pin or paper clip surface, where they bond. The electronegativity, or attraction for chemical bonds, is quite similar between copper (1.9) and iron (1.8). Therefore the copper atoms freely move between these metals.

As an alternative exercise, the electroplating process can be shown with a 9-volt battery. Tape paper clips to the terminals as shown in the experiment for Revelation 14:7 (lesson 76). Now touch one wire (positive battery button) to a penny and the other wire (negative battery button) to the metal object while both are submerged in the vinegar or lemon juice solution. You should observe bubbles and relatively rapid copper plating.

# Night-lights

**Theme:** Creation teaches practical lessons.

**Bible Verse:** But now ask the beasts, and they will teach you; and the birds of the air, and they will tell you; or speak to the earth, and it will teach you; and the fish of the sea will explain to you. (Job 12:7–8)

**Materials Needed:**
- One or more light or glow sticks

## Bible Lesson

Perhaps you have watched fireflies on a warm summer evening. Their soft yellow-green lights blink off and on as they signal each other. Nature is filled with such surprises, and the endless details of creation do not occur by chance or accident. Instead, they show planning and purpose for mankind. It appears that God has placed countless useful ideas in nature that await our discovery. These ideas lead to inventions, new products, and solutions to problems.

Examples of useful designs inspired from nature include the Velcro fastener from cocklebur seeds and aircraft design from bird studies. In this lesson, fireflies teach us how to make colorful night-lights.

Let's give thanks to God for surrounding us with his beautiful and useful designs.

Our Bible verse from Job refers to the clear evidence for creation that surrounds us. The birds, the fish, and the earth itself all show God's handiwork. This lesson suggests a new way to approach science. The study of nature becomes a treasure hunt to discover practical secrets placed there for our enjoyment and benefit.

## Science Activity

Stores sell a large variety of light sticks, or glow sticks, including tubes, bracelets, and necklaces. Each contains two separate liquid chemicals, similar to those formed within the firefly. When the chemicals are mixed together the light turns on. To activate one or more glow lights it is best to darken the room somewhat. You might have someone less familiar with a light stick do the twisting or bending to activate the light. If you have several sticks with multiple colors, so much the better.

It is worth remarking that we cannot compete with the ability of fireflies. Glow sticks typically last a few hours and then fade. Meanwhile, fireflies flash their lights nightly for a week or more.

Light sticks come in a variety of shapes and colors. Fireflies are the inspiration for the design of these portable lights.

## Science Explanation

Just how are fireflies able to glow without batteries or lightbulbs? Their light is variously called cold light, chemical light, or bioluminescence. The action takes place within the firefly abdomen, where two special chemicals are synthesized from their food supply. When mixed, oxygen is combined with one substance, a pigment called luciferin, in the presence of the second chemical, an enzyme called luciferase. Energy from this chemical reaction excites electrons which in turn release visible light.

There are more than two thousand known species of firefly around the world. Their eggs also produce a soft glow, as do the larvae, which are called glowworms. The firefly patterns of flashing light probably are used to communicate and attract mates.

Bioluminescence is very common in the oceans. Almost all deep-sea animals produce chemical lights with various colors. In some cases, luminescent bacteria live inside the marine animals, causing them to glow from the inside out. Creatures on land and in the sea display chemical light, leading to the familiar glow stick.

# The Weight of Air

**Theme:** The Bible is accurate in every single detail, including scientific ideas.

**Bible Verse:** For He looks to the ends of the earth, and sees under the whole heavens, to establish a weight for the wind, and apportion the waters by measure. (Job 28:24–25)

**Materials Needed:**
- Glass of water
- Paper plate or index card
- Hot plate
- Empty soda cans
- Pot holder or tongs
- Tray of cool water

## Bible Lesson

In this technical age it is often assumed that the Bible is outdated and prescientific in its content. After all, Scripture was written more than two thousand years ago, long before modern scientific discoveries. In truth, however, God's Word is found to be entirely accurate, even in the smallest details.

Job 28:24–25 declares that God established the earth's wind and water. The entire chapter describes the source of real wisdom: knowing the Creator who made all things. The "weight [or force] of the wind" is a phrase that accurately describes the heaviness of air. If air had no weight, then the wind could have no force. If this were the case, barometers would read zero pressure. Instead, the air above us exerts an average pressure of 2,100 pounds upon each square foot at the earth's surface, or about 15 pounds per square inch. Job 28, written long before the modern concept of pressure, is entirely correct in referring to the force or weight of the wind. The Bible is indeed trustworthy in every detail.

## Science Activity

There are several ways to demonstrate air pressure or the weight of air. Two interesting methods will be described here. First, fill a glass with water, perhaps from a pitcher. Place a paper plate or index card over the top, and while holding it in place, tip the glass upside down. Now take your hand off the card and it should stay in place. (You may want to do this activity over a sink or dishpan in case of a spill.) The pressure of the air, actually pushing upward from underneath, is greater than the downward weight of the water in the glass. This activity works whether the glass is full or only partially filled with water. You must take care that the paper maintains a good seal, and do not tilt the glass.

The second method requires some preparation ahead of time. Pour one to two inches of water into several empty aluminum soda cans and place them on a hot plate. The water needs to be heated to the point of gently boiling, with steam rising from the openings. When ready, pick up a can with a pot holder or small tongs and tip it upside down into the tray containing shallow water. This will seal the open end of the can below the water level and will also quickly cool the steam inside the can. The activity works best if the water in the tray is cold, perhaps with some ice cubes. As the steam condenses, a vacuum develops within the can. The weight of the outside air will then rapidly crush the can with a loud snapping sound. Repeat the activity with the other cans, or let volunteers try the technique. The weight of the air, referred to in the book of Job, acts as a can crusher.

Water is brought to a boil in a soda can. When the can is inverted in a tray of cold water, it is crushed by air pressure.

## Science Explanation

It may seem that the air is entirely weightless. However, each cubic foot of air actually weighs about one-tenth of a pound. The air in a typical room thus adds up to several hundred pounds.

Air exists for several miles above the earth, gradually thinning with altitude. Gravity keeps this air "attached" to earth. The weight of this air layer is what results in atmospheric pressure on the earth. The pressure exists in all directions; hence, it pushes upward on the card under the glass as well as against the sides of the aluminum cans in the activity.

Why are our bodies not crushed by the ever-present air pressure? We are not affected because we are an "open system." By breathing air, we maintain largely the same pressure inside as outside our bodies. If we dive deeply into water, however, we quickly feel additional pressure from the weight of the water above us.

# Singing Glasses

**Theme:** God gives his children precious comfort in times of trouble.

**Bible Verse:** But no one says, "Where is God my Maker, Who gives songs in the night?" (Job 35:10)

**Materials Needed:**
- Several goblets (or glassware with stems)
- Water

## Bible Lesson

The passage in Job 35 describes those who do not call upon God for help. They may cry out and plead for aid (v. 9), but they ignore the one source of help available to them. Let us be sure that we do not fail in this way. Instead, we have the privilege of calling upon the name of the Lord in times of trouble.

Nights especially can be times of fear and loneliness. This is when the presence of the Lord is most precious, as he "gives songs in the night." Such a song may be a Bible verse or an actual chorus or hymn. Perhaps we take Christian music too much for granted. It is a great blessing; our lives would be diminished without it. Remember Paul and Silas, who were comforted with songs at midnight while they were locked in prison (Acts 16:25). The Lord and his disciples also sang a hymn before they went to the Mount of Olives, where Jesus was arrested (Matthew 26:30).

## Science Activity

Set out several goblets with water in them. Ordinary drinking glasses may also work but not as well. The secret is to have glassware with thin walls.

By themselves the glasses are silent; they have no ability to make music. However, the touch of a finger can make them sing. Wet your index finger and gently stroke the goblet completely and continuously around the rim while you hold the glass steady by the base of the stem. Very little finger pressure is needed, and the finger must be kept moist while it is moving around the rim. In a few seconds the glass should start to resonate or vibrate, causing a clear, loud sound. The ringing sound is quite pleasant. The pitch, or frequency, depends on the glass size and also on the amount of water it contains. Volunteers may want to help you get several goblets vibrating at the same time. By adjusting the water levels, interesting chords can be produced. It takes a gentle hand to coax the sounds from the glasses. Likewise, it takes the Lord to give comforting "songs in the night."

A moist finger rubbed around the rim can cause a goblet to ring.

## Science Explanation

The ringing of a glass is called a resonance vibration. Sound is always produced by vibrating objects, whether violin strings, vocal cords, or air currents within a flute. For a goblet, the moving finger causes the sides of the glass to vibrate slightly inward and outward. The moistened finger provides a smooth contact, necessary for the continuous sound. It is somewhat like a violin bow moving across a string and causing the string to vibrate.

The sound produced by a goblet has a frequency of several hundred cycles per second. If you watch the water surface closely, you will see tiny standing waves produced by the moving glass walls.

Goblets can sometimes be shattered by high-frequency sounds that originate outside themselves. This is also called resonance, but it is an entirely different type of vibration. The shattering frequency is well above 20,000 cycles per second and very intense. In this case, the atoms within the glass begin to vibrate violently and eventually tear apart, resulting in breakage. There is no danger of broken glass in our activity as long as one holds the goblet upright.

If you have difficulty getting sound from the glassware, it may help to wet your fingertip with vinegar. The vinegar dissolves any oil that may be present and increases the needed friction between your fingertip and the glass rim.

# Through a Lens

**Theme:** Creation evidence is always before our eyes.

**Bible Verse:** Remember to magnify His work, of which men have sung. (Job 36:24)

**Materials Needed:**
- Newspaper page
- Needle-nose pliers
- Paper clips
- Water

## Bible Lesson

Job experienced many afflictions from Satan. During this time of testing, three friends or "comforters" came to discuss Job's condition. Another friend, Elihu, speaks in Job 36. This chapter describes God's control of nature, especially details of the weather. Elihu counsels Job to extol or magnify the works of creation. This means to make great, to emphasize, and to concentrate on God's marvelous works. Everyone can see the evidence of God in creation as declared in verse 25: "Everyone has seen it; man looks on it from afar." Commentary writer Matthew Henry wrote three centuries ago concerning creation, "Every man that has but half an eye may see it." Nevertheless, many people today do not acknowledge God's presence in the creation. Foolishly they choose to ignore the evidence that surrounds them. Romans 1:20 declares that there is no valid excuse for ignoring God's works in this way. Life is filled with choices, and the choices we make have consequences. We must be sure we choose to honor the Lord who makes all things, including ourselves.

## Science Activity

The Dutch scientist Anton van Leeuwenhoek lived from 1632 to 1723. He is known as the father of microbiology because he applied the microscope to the living world. The instrument had been invented some decades earlier by Hans Lippershey (1570–1619). Some early magnifiers used lenses made of droplets of water. Participants in this lesson will make a similar magnifier to illustrate the early exploration of the microscopic world.

A paper clip needs to be partially straightened. Then a small closed loop (about ⅛ inch across) is twisted at the end using needle-nose pliers, as shown. Now dip the loop into water so that a thin droplet remains suspended within the metal loop. Hold this loop directly above some small print and observe the writing through the droplet. The water layer may either increase or decrease the size of the letters, depending on the droplet's shape. To make the water drop a magnifier, gently rub the wire loop across the lip of the water container to remove excess water.

The water lens magnifies small objects because of the curvature of the water surface. Large permanent lenses of similar shape usually are made of clear glass or plastic. Microscopes of many varieties explore the smallest details of nature. The wonders of creation are found to extend from the vast galaxies to the smallest atoms.

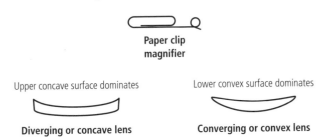

**Paper clip**
**magnifier**

Upper concave surface dominates

**Diverging or concave lens**

Lower convex surface dominates

**Converging or convex lens**

A paper clip becomes a magnifier when straightened and given a small loop at the end. Shown is a diverging lens that demagnifies and also a converging lens that magnifies an object.

## Science Explanation

A lens changes the apparent size of an object by refracting or bending the light reflected from the object. Lenses can be either *converging* or *diverging* in shape.

A diverging or concave lens has at least one surface that curves inward. An object sighted through this lens appears smaller than actual size. In our experiment this decrease in size occurs when extra water is present within the wire loop. The bottom surface will always bulge downward, but the top water surface may be concave. This concave top surface dominates for a diverging lens.

A converging or convex lens has surfaces that are bowed more outward than inward. An object viewed through a convex lens is magnified. In this case the upper water surface in the loop may still be bowed slightly inward, but the bottom downward bulge dominates.

# Swirling Clouds

**Theme:** God controls the weather.

**Bible Verse:** He causes it [weather details] to come, whether for correction, or for His land, or for mercy. (Job 37:13)

**Materials Needed:**
- Clear drinking glasses
- Water
- Ink or food coloring

## Bible Lesson

Weather is more commonly talked about than any other topic. The weather itself and the forecasters who bravely try to predict it are also the targets of many complaints. Job 37 gives a clear description of the many ingredients that can make up our daily weather: thunder and lightning (vv. 1–5), rain and snow (vv. 6–8), and wind and clouds (vv. 9–12). Verse 13 gives some basic reasons why God sends storms. For example, they may bring correction, as in the time of Noah. Storms may also bring needed moisture to the land. Lightning replenishes the soil with nitrogen so that crops can be produced. God's love is constantly shown as the earth is cared for and refreshed by the variety in the weather.

Job himself was no stranger to storms. A firestorm had burned up his sheep and servants (Job 1:16). Then a mighty wind suddenly killed all ten of his children (Job 1:19). Even then Job honored the Lord with these words: "The LORD gave, and the LORD has taken away; Blessed be the name of the LORD" (Job 1:21).

Job realized that God controls all the details of nature, including the weather. Perhaps we are too quick to complain about the heat, cold, and storms. God surely has his reasons for the weather, either rain or shine.

## Science Activity

Participants will observe the unusual mixing of two liquids. Completely fill the drinking glasses with water; then let the water settle and become still for at least one minute. Several people can observe each glass. Gently place two or three drops of ink or food coloring on the top surface of the water. The dye is slightly heavier than water and will slowly sink. As the dye settles, it should form a small ring within the water. This ring will in turn separate into still smaller rings, and so on. Place more dye on the water's surface to repeat the intriguing process.

The unusual behavior of the moving dye illustrates the complex motion and mixing of air masses in the sky. Such atmospheric mixing does not form simple rings as observed here. Instead, there are a large number of complex interactions continually occurring in the atmosphere.

The rings and turbulence observed within the glass of water are not completely understood by scientists. It is no wonder that weather forecasters are not always successful in their daily predictions. Only the Lord knows completely the details of tomorrow's weather.

## Science Explanation

The sinking dye illustrates Daniel Bernoulli's principle (1738). This rule states that the pressure of a fluid decreases with increased velocity of the fluid. As the ring of dye settles in the water, the outer portion slows down slightly. This causes a slow rotation of the entire ring.

Dye (ink or food coloring) settling in water develops a multiple-ring appearance.

Turning speed is greater within the dye ring, so the inside pressure is smaller and the ring holds together. Similar pressure differences may lead to the stability of tornadoes and hurricanes.

Instabilities within the sinking ring of dye soon lead to breakup, followed by several smaller rings. This process continues indefinitely until ended by the bottom of the glass or dilution of the dye. The observed motion of the dye is a combination of streamlined and turbulent fluid flow. This process has not yet been exactly duplicated by computer models. Complex fluid motions are some of the many unsolved mysteries of science.

# Numbers in Nature

**Theme:** Created patterns show God's fingerprint.

**Bible Verse:** Where were you when I laid the foundations of the earth? Tell Me, if you have understanding. (Job 38:4)

**Materials Needed:**
- Flowers
- Other available items mentioned in the lesson
- Pinecones and pine needles

## Bible Lesson

Job suffered greatly at the hand of Satan. He lost his children, his health, and his possessions. Most of the book of Job describes the unsuccessful efforts of his friends to comfort him. But in chapter 38, God speaks to Job from a whirlwind, asking a series of profound questions. Job is made to realize that God's ways are sometimes "past finding out." In his wisdom, God allows circumstances to happen that we cannot understand from this side of heaven.

In our Bible verse, God asks Job if he was present at the creation. Of course, the answer is no—for Job and for all of mankind. This answer implies that we should not attempt to second-guess exactly how God accomplished creation. In fact, this supernatural event is completely beyond our grasp. The laying of the earth's foundation describes God's careful planning of the earth. The next verse describes the marking off of the earth's dimensions. In other words, mathematical precision was part of the creation details. And still today, arithmetic patterns are found throughout nature.

Job did not have all the answers of life, but he knew that God cared for him even more than the physical creation. Job's testimony of trust in God, recorded in Job 1:21, should also be ours. It includes the words, "The LORD gave and the LORD has taken away; blessed be the name of the LORD."

## Science Activity

This activity begins with an arithmetic puzzle. On a sheet of paper, blackboard, or screen, write the following numbers and blanks:

1, 1, 2, 3, _____, _____

Ask volunteers to guess the next two missing numbers. Some will correctly guess 5 and 8, each found by adding the two previous numbers in the list, $2 + 3 = 5$ and $3 + 5 = 8$. This number sequence continues indefinitely. It is called the *Fibonacci sequence* of numbers, named for the mathematician Leonardo Fibonacci (pronounced fee'-ba-na-chee) of Pisa who lived eight centuries ago.

Now explain that these particular numbers are very common in nature. They frequently occur in the studies of plants and animals. For example, flower petals often come in clusters of 5 or 8. Flower species with 4, 6, or 7 petals can be found, but they occur less often. Pass several objects around the audience or show pictures to a larger group and have them look for Fibonacci numbers. Here are several examples:

Pine needle clusters almost always grow in clusters of two, three, or five needles.

A typical cloverleaf has three petals. Four-leaf clovers exist, but they are mutations or mistakes and are infrequent.

A sand dollar from the sea displays a star pattern with five points on its surface. Most starfish also have five arms.

An apple cut in half will display a five-pointed star in its center.

When counted, the petals of most flower blossoms number five, eight, or higher.

If pinecones are available, the number of distinct spirals around the outside can be counted. The number is very likely 5, 8, or 13. The surface of a pineapple gives similar results. Why does this Fibonacci number pattern appear in nature more often than not? There is no convincing evolutionary explanation. Instead, we see a pattern that the Lord chose to imprint on his works. Creation is not random or accidental but instead shows intelligent design. Challenge the audience to be on the lookout for Fibonacci numbers in nature.

Fibonacci numbers are illustrated by three-leaf clovers, flower petals, sand dollars, pine needles, and pinecones.

## Science Explanation

Leonardo Fibonacci (1175–1230) is also known as Leonardo of Pisa. During medieval times he made many mathematical discoveries. He is best known for the number sequence that bears his name. After the first two numbers, future entries are generated by the formula

$$S_n = S_{n-1} + S_{n-2} \quad n \geq 3$$

That is, the next number is the sum of the two preceding numbers. Fibonacci's initial application of these numbers was to explain the birth pattern of generations of rabbits. This is discussed in many math texts.

The Fibonacci numbers rapidly become large: 1, 1, 2, 3, 5, 8, 13, 21, 34, 55, 89, 144, 233, 377, 610, 987, 1597, and so on. It is more of a challenge to locate the larger numbers in nature, but they do appear. The study of geometric and numerical patterns in plants is called *phyllotaxis*. The following list gives many Fibonacci examples from plants and trees.

| | |
|---|---|
| Aster | 21 petals |
| Buttercup | 5 petals |
| Chicory | 21 petals |
| Daisy | Spirals in core of blossom number 21 and 34; petals typically number 34, 55, or 89 |
| Delphinium | 8 petals |
| Eastern white pine | Clusters of 5 needles |
| Enchanter's nightshade | 2 petals |
| Iris | 3 petals |
| Ivy | 3 leaves |
| Larch conifer | Cone has 5 spirals in one direction, 8 in another |
| Lily | 3 petals |
| Lodgepole pine | Clusters of 2 needles |
| Marigold | 13 petals |
| Michaelmas daisy | 89 petals |
| Norway spruce | Cone has 3 spirals in one direction, 5 in another |
| Oxalis | 3 petals |
| Periwinkle | 5 petals |

| | |
|---|---|
| Pineapple | Diamond-shaped surface spirals number 8 and 13 in two directions |
| Plantain | 34 petals |
| Ponderosa pine | Clusters of 3 needles |
| Primrose | 5 petals |
| Pyrethrum | 34 petals |
| Red pine | Clusters of 2 needles |
| Sunflower | Spirals of seeds in the flower, depending on the species, number 21 and 34, 34 and 55, 55 and 89, or 89 and 144. |
| Trillium | 3 petals |
| Virginia creeper | 5 leaves |

There are also exceptions to Fibonacci numbers in nature, including these:

| | |
|---|---|
| African violet | 4 petals |
| Clematis | 6 petals |
| Flowering dogwood | 4 petals |
| Honeycomb | 6-sided hexagons |
| Lilac | 4 petals |
| Magnolia blossom | 6 petals |
| Snowflake | 6 points |

The Fibonacci sequence has many additional interesting properties. For example, the ratio of any two adjacent, larger Fibonacci numbers approaches the *golden mean*, or 1.618. The fraction $^{1597}/_{987}$ is close to this number, which is sometimes also called the *divine proportion*. Rectangular objects with a length-to-width ratio of about 1 to 1.6 are especially pleasing to the eye. The Greek Pantheon was built with its length and width based on this ratio. Many breakfast cereal boxes are also designed with these dimensions in mind to attract our attention. It is also no accident that the piano has an eight-note octave with five black keys and eight white keys.

Fibonacci numbers are embedded everywhere in the fabric of art and science. Mathematics is the language of creation, and these numbers are one example. Today there is an international association dedicated to the mathematical study of Fibonacci numbers. Their journal is called the *Fibonacci Quarterly*.

# Keeping in Balance

**Theme:** God provides stability in a changing world.

**Bible Verse:** I have set the LORD always before me; because He is at my right hand I shall not be moved. (Psalm 16:8)

**Materials Needed:**
- Yardstick or broom
- Long pencils or rulers for participants

## Bible Lesson

Psalm 16 describes the confidence David experienced in his life. He faced many severe problems, yet he still wrote this wonderful testimony. With the Lord at his side, David could not be moved or shaken. This means there was not the slightest danger of losing his position in Christ. Nor could he ever be disappointed with his decision to follow the Lord. David had tied his life to a secure refuge that would not fail. In this turbulent world we too can enjoy confidence in the Lord as David did. The promise of our key verse is repeated by Peter in Acts 2:25.

## Science Activity

Demonstrate a technique for balancing objects in an unusual manner by holding the broom or yardstick horizontally for all to see. Rest it upon your two index fingers. Begin with the fingers widely separated for easy support of the stick. Now comes the interesting part: slowly slide your fingers inward toward each other. It is okay if one finger slides more than the other. When the fingers meet, the stick should remain horizontal and perfectly balanced. This balance point will be at the center of the yardstick and somewhat off center for the broom. Your fingers will automatically seek this position, also known as the object's center of gravity.

Participants can easily repeat this balancing act with pencils or rulers. Have them support the item on their index fingers. The initial position of the fingers is not important. Then have them slide their fingers inward—the balance point is automatically found.

Now lock in the lesson idea. Emphasize that the Lord can keep our lives in balance. We all face daily pressures, temptations, and disappointments. These things can quickly throw us off balance and interfere with our Christian walk. But here is the good news: Christ can bring our lives back into balance. His power helped David and is still available today. Confidence in the Lord automatically provides us with a balance point in our lives.

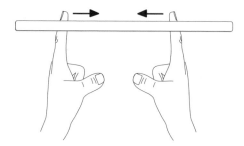

A stick of any length has a balance point, located by moving both fingers inward until they touch.

## Science Explanation

Every object has a center of gravity. This activity locates the balance point by sliding one's fingers inward while supporting the object. With a broom or ruler, the finger closer to the balance point supports most of the weight. This results in more friction and less ability to slide; the other finger slides instead. When the fingers are supporting equal weight, either they will both slide or they will alternate in motion. It is always the finger with less friction that slides. The differences are automatically sorted out by friction until the fingers meet at the balance point.

# Blue Skies and Red Sunsets

**Theme:** God's colorful artwork fills the skies.

**Bible Verse:** The heavens declare the glory of God; and the firmament shows His handiwork. (Psalm 19:1)

**Materials Needed:**
- Flashlight
- Large clear drinking glass or pitcher
- Drops of milk or powdered coffee creamer

## Bible Lesson

We are surrounded by the beauty of God's creation. On each new day it is easy to take many details for granted, including the clouds, blue skies, and breezes. Psalm 19 reminds us that God's creative work is everywhere, including the skies above. Day after day the sky shows its glorious colors: bright blue by day, red and orange hues at sunrise and sunset. On the moon, in contrast, there is no air and therefore no sky color. The lunar skies are continually black, both night and day.

In nature studies there need not be a separation of science from the Bible. These two sources of knowledge work together and reinforce each other. For example, while science explains the technical formation of sky colors, Scripture explains their purpose, which is to show God's glory and planning in the details of creation. It is God who has filled the earth with objects that are pleasant to our sight (see Genesis 2:9). Even cameras cannot fully capture the artwork of God.

## Science Activity

We will illustrate how blue skies and red sunsets occur. Fill the clear container with water. Shine the flashlight through the side of the container; the beam may or may not be visible. Now mix a small amount of milk or powdered creamer into the water. The light beam should now become visible, whether or not the room is darkened. From the side the beam should be slightly blue in color. When facing the beam where it leaves the water, there should be a slight yellow appearance to the light. As more milk or powder is added to the water, the colors intensify somewhat.

The white light is partially separated into its component colors by particles in the water. The blue color is more readily "scattered" and turns the length of flashlight beam to a blue-gray color. This is similar to the blue sky that results when sunlight passes through the air. The white flashlight beam, minus the color blue, gives the slight yellow color. During sunrise and sunset, color separation is extreme and the sun becomes orange or red in appearance. The colors of our indoor experiment cannot compare with the brilliant colors of the actual sun and sky.

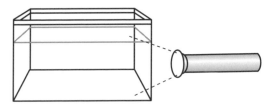

Small particles of milk in water will separate light into its component colors.

## Science Explanation

Blue skies and red sunsets arise from the scattering of sunlight. The process was first explained by British scientists Lord Rayleigh and John Tyndall in the late 1800s. The sun's light waves are absorbed by air molecules and then emitted again an instant later. The blue color, with a shorter wavelength than red, is more readily scattered across the sky. When the sun is low on the horizon at morning or evening, its light passes through additional air molecules and the red color now begins to scatter. Therefore the bright orange-red colors are often seen at sunrise or sunset.

The complicated process by which air molecules scatter sunlight is not fully understood by scientists. However, this display of God's artwork in the sky can be enjoyed by all.

# Music of the Spheres

**Theme:** Planets obey God's laws of motion.

**Bible Verse:** The heavens declare the glory of God; and the firmament shows His handiwork. (Psalm 19:1)

**Materials Needed:**
- Cardboard or corkboard sheets
- Lengths of string
- Sheets of plain paper, the bigger the better
- Thumbtacks or straight pins

## Bible Lesson

Evidence of planning and design in creation surrounds us. From the very smallest objects to the largest, from atoms to galaxies, the fingerprint of God may be clearly seen on all levels. In this lesson we will consider the motions of the planets.

For many centuries the movement of planets across the night sky was a great mystery. These space objects did not follow the regular nightly motion of the background stars. Instead, as weeks or months passed, the planets slowly wandered through the background of stars. The word *planet* itself means "wanderer." During the 1600s the German astronomer Johannes Kepler carefully studied the planetary motion of Mars. He discovered several basic rules that govern all planets as they orbit the sun. Today these results are known as Kepler's laws. He was deeply impressed by the regular, predictable motion of the planets, and he compared their motion with the regular vibrations of musical instruments. Kepler imagined the planets to be creating celestial music by their regular cycles around the sun. Kepler poetically called planetary motion the "music of the spheres," a term from ancient Greek times. The well-known hymn "This Is My Father's World" refers to this heavenly music:

> All nature sings and round me rings
> The music of the spheres.

At an earlier time it was thought that planetary motion was random and unpredictable. However, Kepler found that the planets move dependably and that they fit the description of Psalm 19:1, just as every other part of the creation does.

## Science Activity

The curved paths of planets around the sun can be drawn by individuals or small teams of two to three people. Place a blank sheet of paper on a cardboard or corkboard surface. Then insert two thumbtacks or pins through the paper and into the cardboard as shown. Tie the ends of a string together to make a loop and place it loosely over the thumbtacks. Now draw a curved line on the paper, constrained by the limits of the string. A smooth, egg-shaped curve should result, called an ellipse. An ellipse is somewhat like a flattened circle with two centers at the pin locations, called the focus points.

The planets revolve about the sun in vast orbits with elliptical shapes. The sun is positioned at one of the focus points, shown in the drawing. Participants can experiment by moving the pins closer together or farther apart. These positions respectively give nearly circular orbits and greatly elongated, narrow curves. Ellipse drawing may also be demonstrated on a whiteboard or blackboard. Use small pieces of tape to hold the ends of the string and then draw the curve.

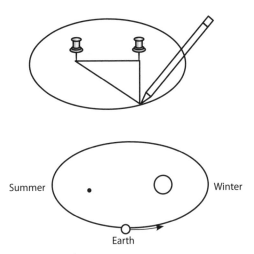

An ellipse can be drawn using a loop of string, two thumbtacks, and a pen or pencil. The lower figure illustrates the earth's orbit around the sun, not drawn to scale. All planet orbits are elliptical in shape.

## Science Explanation

All orbiting planets, moons, and comets move along elliptical paths. This is due to the nature of the gravity force. As the illustration shows, planets move closer and then farther from the sun during their annual orbit. In the Northern Hemisphere, the earth is actually a bit closer to the sun during winter, 91 million miles, compared to 95 million miles in summer. It is the tilt of the earth that largely controls our seasons, not the distance changes.

Kepler's three laws of planetary motion are expressed as follows:

1. Orbits are ellipses.
2. Planets sweep out equal areas in equal times. That is, they slow down somewhat when farther from the sun (aphelion) and speed up when closer to the sun (perihelion).
3. The orbit time T for a planet varies with its average solar distance R by the relation $T^2 = R^3$.

The ellipses drawn in this activity have various shapes or *eccentricities*. Eccentricity is defined as the separation distance of the focus points divided by the maximum diameter of the resulting ellipse. A perfect circle has zero eccentricity since the two focus points overlap. A narrow ellipse has a high eccentricity, approaching the maximum value of one. The following table lists actual eccentricities for various objects in the solar system:

| Solar system member | Eccentricity of orbit |
|---|---|
| Venus | 0.007 |
| Earth | 0.017 |
| Moon | 0.055 |
| Mars | 0.093 |
| Pluto | 0.249 |
| Halley's Comet | 0.900 |

The earth's orbit is nearly circular, while that of Pluto and Halley's Comet are quite narrow and elongated.

# Bad Habits

**Theme:** Make sure your habits are positive so they will be a strength rather than a weakness, and rely on God's strength to break bad habits.

**Bible Verses:** Cleanse me from secret faults. Keep back Your servant also from presumptuous sins; let them not have dominion over me. (Psalm 19:12–13)

**Materials Needed:**
- Roll of masking tape or adding machine paper
- Volunteer

## Bible Lesson

David prayed that God would forgive and protect him from two kinds of sin: "hidden faults" and "presumptuous sins." Hidden faults are problems that we may not be aware of. These weaknesses, or bad habits, can become such a part of our lives that we don't notice their effects. Presumptuous sin is disobedience that we are aware of and make a conscious decision about. Either kind of sin is a failing before God that needs our confession and his forgiveness, just as David prayed.

## Science Activity

This lesson calls for a volunteer to stand before the group. A roll of tape represents a fault or problem. Wrap the tape around the person a couple of times, with his or her arms down. Ask the person to break loose from the "fault," which is easily done by spreading their arms and breaking the ribbon of tape.

When a sin is repeated often, however, it becomes a habit that is hard to break. Repeatedly wrap the tape around the person's arms while you talk, ten or twenty times around. Again ask the person to break free, but this will prove a more difficult task than before. The small strength of each individual section of tape now combines with the others to add up to a confining barrier. Likewise, bad habits can completely take over a person's life. Finally, carefully cut through the strands with scissors to represent God's power through prayer. We can have freedom from bad habits with the Lord's help.

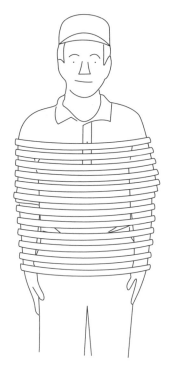

A person can be tied up with many coils of tape.

## Science Explanation

A single strip of masking tape or paper tape can be broken easily like a thread, especially by snapping it. Suppose, however, that a person is wrapped twenty times around by the tape. It will take twenty times as much force to break loose, and the snapping motion is no longer possible.

Many small sections add up to a strong barrier. Further investigation of strong cords or ropes will show that they are made up of weak individual threads. As Ecclesiastes 4:12 reminds us in a positive way, a cord of three strands is not quickly broken.

# The Lord's Strength

**Theme:** When we are on the Lord's side, his strength is available to us.

**Bible Verse:** God is our refuge and strength, a very present help in trouble. (Psalm 46:1)

**Materials Needed:**
- Length of rope about 25 feet long
- Two sturdy broomsticks, poles, or PVC pipes
- Two or more volunteers

## Bible Lesson

People are very interested in improving their health and strength. Physical fitness centers prosper almost everywhere. These efforts are commendable, but physical strength is only temporary. How quickly it fades with age.

In contrast, the Lord's strength is permanent and readily available to us. This does not necessarily mean he gives us the ability to win races or lift weights. Instead, God's refuge and strength help us to have victory over the pressures of life. When troubles arise, the Christian has spiritual resources that include prayer, the Bible, and Christian friends. By trusting in Christ, we exchange our own limited strength for that of the Creator of the entire universe.

## Science Activity

This activity shows how one person's strength can be greatly increased. It reminds us of extra strength that is available from the Lord. The activity requires at least two volunteers. You will show that you are stronger than both of them combined.

Have the two volunteers stand facing one another, each holding a sturdy broom or pole. After tying one end of a smooth rope (one that slides easily) to one of the broomsticks, loop it around both sticks several times, keeping them about two feet apart. Now have the volunteers pull outward on the broomsticks. When you pull steadily on the free end of the rope the sticks should be drawn together, regardless of how hard your volunteers resist. The feat should also work well with four volunteers pulling against you.

You have actually made a block and tackle system, long used to gain what is called a mechanical advantage. Your pulling force is multiplied

Two broomstricks are loosely wrapped with rope. One person can outpull several others by pulling on the end of the rope to draw the sticks together.

by the number of loops around the broomsticks; your volunteers don't have a chance. With a strong rope and the right arrangement of pulleys, it is possible to pull a car up a hill or even to pull down a tree. Just as you gain an advantage with the rope, the Lord's strength gives an advantage during difficult times.

## Science Explanation

Suppose you and the four volunteers can each pull with a force of fifty pounds. Each broomstick will then be pulled outward with one hundred pounds. If there are five turns of rope around the sticks, your force will be multiplied to 250 pounds (5 x 50). Thus you have a 150-pound advantage. Some of this advantage will be lost due to the friction of the rope. If this loss is small, you can still easily outpull the volunteers.

Notice that two of the four volunteers are not really necessary. The experiment would be the same if one broomstick were permanently attached to a wall. By Newton's third law of motion, the wall will pull back (reaction) with a force equal to that of the volunteers (action force). However, the four struggling volunteers give a more impressive appearance.

This activity does not defy the conservation or constancy of energy. Instead, the advantage of a greater force is gained at the expense of a longer length of pull. As you draw the two broomsticks together, you will accumulate a coil of rope at your feet.

# Seeing Upside Down

**Theme:** Eyesight is a precious gift from God.

**Bible Verse:** He who planted the ear, shall He not hear? He who formed the eye, shall He not see? (Psalm 94:9)

**Materials Needed:**
- Glass or plastic magnifying lenses, or clear marbles.
- White cards

## Bible Lesson

God has clearly designed the blessing of eyesight. Consider just a few of the details that make our vision possible. First, the eye is recessed into its socket and well protected by surrounding bones. Otherwise the sensitive eye surface could be easily injured. Second, the eyebrow and eyelash provide an umbrella-like shield from rain and dust. Third, our blinking process and eye fluid act like a windshield wiper and washer to keep the outer cornea moist and healthy.

As we enter the interior of the eye, the complexity increases greatly. An image is focused by the cornea and lens onto the retina at the rear of the eyeball. This retina is covered with millions of tiny light sensors called rods and cones. The result is that our eye functions as a color

109

video camera with automatic focusing and clear image storage in the brain. This divinely created mechanism is advanced far beyond any modern optical device.

The eye lens itself deserves special attention. Made of clear gelatin-like material, the lens is flexible in its shape. This allows us to focus on nearby objects as the lens becomes thicker and distant objects as the lens slightly thins. This continuous flexing of the lens occurs automatically. As light from an object passes through the lens, it meets the retina in inverted fashion. Thus everything we see is initially upside down. When the visual signal reaches the brain through the optic nerve, it is then corrected so that we can see normally and right side up.

Psalm 94:9 reminds us that God formed the eye in his wisdom. Such wonderful senses as sight and hearing do not arise by chance. Further, the One who made our eyes in the first place can surely see all of his creation, including our inner hearts. This should be a fearful thought to those not living for the Lord. For believers, however, it is a precious truth that God knows all our ways and he still loves us beyond measure.

## Science Activity

We will explore the upside-down nature of lenses. Each participant needs to be supplied with an inexpensive magnifying lens. The lens is held up to a distant window or light. Then the image of the window or light source is found by using a white card as a small screen behind the lens. Look closely at the focused image on the card and you should notice that it is inverted. If held several inches from the eye, the lens can be looked through directly instead of using the card. Eyes, cameras, and telescopes likewise record an upside-down image in this way.

If the lens is held close to an object—for example, to read fine print—the image will be right side up and enlarged. This magnified image cannot be projected onto a card.

Depending on distance, lenses commonly turn images upside down because of the laws of optics. Knowing this, God also provided a correcting mechanism within our brains so we can see right side up. This vision process works automatically without our concern or understanding. Many of us need the corrective help of glasses, contact lenses, or eye surgery. Even when eyesight is imperfect, however, it is still a precious gift from God.

If lenses are not available, one can use a clear marble. Hold the marble close to your eye and look at a distant object, which will appear upside down.

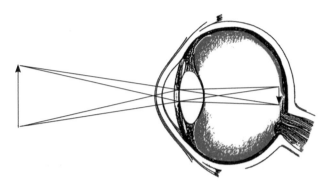

Light passes through the cornea and lens of the eye and then forms an inverted image on the retina.

## Science Explanation

The figure shows an eye focused on an arrow. As light rays reflected from the arrow pass through the eye's outer cornea and lens, they are bent or refracted. The result is a clear inverted image on the retina. All the light rays coming from the top of the arrow, for example, meet at the same place on the lower part of the retina.

The human eye lens is somewhat flexible, changing shape for different distances. In looking at the moon, for example, the eye lens becomes thinner. In contrast, to view nearby objects clearly the lens becomes slightly thicker. This flexing process is called *accommodation*. Muscles arranged around the lens make this possible. When these muscles become fatigued, it is time to close one's eyes to give them a rest.

No cameras yet are made with a lens that changes its shape. Instead, cameras rely on lens movement inward or outward, or actual lens replacement. With its adjustable lens, the human eye is the most advanced camera known, coming from the hands of the Master Designer.

If time permits, further exploration can be done with two lenses. Hold one close to your eye and the other farther outward. Look through *both* lenses at once, with the same eye, at a distant object.

This is a challenge but can be done. Move the distant lens outward or inward until a clear image is seen. If the lens close to your eye is thicker than the second lens, the image should be somewhat magnified. What you now have made is one of the great inventions of all time, the refracting telescope. Galileo first constructed such a device from two lenses four centuries ago, around 1610. With his primitive telescope, Galileo observed craters on the moon, the rings of Saturn, Jupiter's moons, and many other wonders in the night sky.

# Rapid Growth

**Theme:** God cares for his creatures.

**Bible Verse:** He causes the grass to grow for the cattle, and vegetation for the service of man, that he may bring forth food from the earth. (Psalm 104:14)

**Materials Needed:**
- Sheets of paper of various sizes

## Bible Lesson

Psalm 104 has been called the "ecologist's psalm." Ecology is the study of living things and their environments. The psalm wonderfully describes all aspects of creation, including springs of water, trees, storks, wild goats, the moon, lions, sea creatures, and volcanoes. A recurring theme of the psalm is that God cares for the daily needs of his creatures. Verse 14 describes the provision of food for both man and beast.

In 1838, Charles Darwin (1809–82) read an essay by Thomas Malthus titled "On the Principle of Population." Malthus argued that humans and animals always outgrow their food supply. If true, this inevitably leads to intense competition and mass starvation. Malthus assumed that over time populations grow *geometrically* (2, 4, 8, 16, 32, etc.) while food supplies, at best, grow *arithmetically* (2, 4, 6, 8, 10, etc.). Darwin was strongly influenced by the pessimistic predictions of Malthus, and this became the false basis for his theories of mutation, competition, and natural selection for the formation and improvement of species.

This idea is challenged today by the dual trends of limited human population growth and abundant food supplies. Regional food shortages today are due to conflicts and distribution problems, not a worldwide lack of food. The threat of future food crises is also dispelled by Psalm 104:14. In truth, God continues to care for the physical needs of his creatures.

## Science Activity

The term *geometric* or *exponential* growth is mentioned in the Bible lesson. This type of increase starts out gradually and then rapidly escalates as the numbers continue to double. Charles Darwin misapplied geometric growth, but it is a fascinating type of change. Many items in nature and in our culture increase geometrically:

Computer memory capacity

Food production

Growth of principal with compound interest

Information

Total number of books published

We will demonstrate geometric growth with a paper-folding exercise. Begin by asking participants to estimate how many times they can continue to fold a sheet of paper in half. One might suppose the number is almost limitless with an ever smaller result. However, it is practically impossible to fold any paper more than 6 to 8 times, regardless of its original size. This is true of writing paper, newspaper, or tissues. Consider the increasing number of paper thicknesses with repeated folding: 1, 2, 4, 8, 16, 32, 64, 128, 256, 512, 1,024, 2,048 . . . After just six foldings there are 64 paper thicknesses, equal to a major portion of this book, and any further folding becomes very difficult.

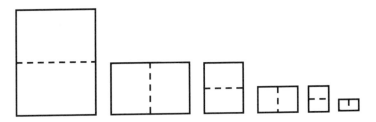

Any size sheet of paper can be folded only 6 to 8 times. The paper thickness doubles with each fold.

## Science Explanation

Our geometric growth example can be written as $2^n$, where n is the number of paper foldings. Some larger, theoretical numbers of foldings are summarized in the table.

Geometric growth can be applied in a positive way to evangelism. Suppose a believer shares the gospel with two other people. Each of these two then share with two others, and so on. The number of people exposed to the gospel will then increase according to the number sequence seen earlier: 2, 4, 8, 16, 32, 64 . . . After just 32 "levels," the entire world population would be reached. In this day of nearly instant communication with social media, the possibility of worldwide outreach is exciting.

| Number of folds ($n$) | Total sheets of thickness | Approximate total thickness |
|:---:|:---:|:---:|
| 5 | 32 | 0.125 in. |
| 10 | 1024 | 4 in. |
| 15 | 32,768 | 10.7 ft. |
| 20 | 1.05 million | 341 ft. |
| 25 | 33.5 million | 2 miles |
| 30 | 1 billion | 17,000 miles |
| 35 | 32 billion | 1 million miles |

# Amplifying Sound

**Theme:** God gifted us with an impressive and complex hearing system.

**Bible Verse:** I will praise You, for I am fearfully and wonderfully made; marvelous are Your works, and that my soul knows very well. (Psalm 139:14)

**Materials Needed:**
- Sheets of paper
- Tape
- Straight pins
- Fine-grain sandpaper

## Bible Lesson

David was deeply impressed by the creation of life, as each of us should be. In our day, however, ideas contrary to creation abound, such as evolutionary origin and slow improvement through random mutations. David's testimony is a refreshing and timely contrast to such false ideas.

As just one example of creative design, consider our sense of hearing. Our ears allow us to enjoy birds and musical instruments, voices and songs. Hearing also protects us by warning of approaching danger.

The assumed evolution of the ear has not been explained in detail. Somehow our animal ancestors are said to have developed open canals beneath their skin, along with cells sensitive to sound vibrations. But consider the complex sequence of vibrations that must work together perfectly when one hears a sound. The sequence of sound vibrations moves through each of these objects in turn:

Violin string

Air molecules

Outer eardrum

Hammer, anvil, stirrup (the three smallest bones in our bodies)

Inner eardrum

Fluid within the ear's cochlea

Hair follicles lining the cochlea

Electrons within nerves at the base of the follicles

The brain circuitry itself

When the vibrating electric signal finally reaches the brain, we hear beautiful music. All this happens in a split second, and with vibrations of hundreds or thousands of cycles per second.

How could such a complex system evolve over time and completely by chance? All the details of the ear must be present and working together for hearing to exist; the ear simply could not develop haphazardly or slowly. Similar examples of God's intricate design can be seen throughout our bodies and the entire creation. Evolutionary alternatives to David's testimony are neither convincing nor scientifically satisfying.

## Science Activity

This activity explores the definition of sound as a vibration. A simple sound amplifier can be made with a sheet of paper and a straight pin. Roll the paper into a cone and tape it. An opening is not necessary at the tip; uneven paper at the flared end does not matter. Now reach inside and push the pin through the narrow end so the pin point protrudes outward to the side (not through the tip).

Hold the cone and pull the pin across any object; it will vibrate and the paper megaphone should amplify the sound. Try rubbing the pin across cloth, sandpaper, or any other rough surface. A static sound will result as the pin vibrates unevenly.

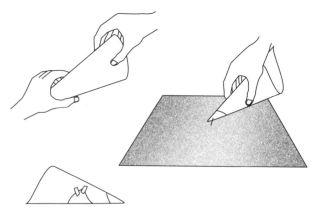

A homemade paper loudspeaker will amplify sound.

## Science Explanation

Sound can be defined as a vibration, whether caused by a violin string, a drum, or a person's vocal cords. In this experiment the pin vibrates rapidly by passing over a rough surface. The paper cone attached to the pin also vibrates. The greater size of the cone then causes nearby air molecules to vibrate. This air pressure disturbance finally reaches our eardrums. The cone is somewhat similar to an audio speaker inside a radio or television.

# Hot or Cold?

**Theme:** We cannot always trust our own judgment.

**Bible Verse:** Trust in the Lord with all your heart, and lean not on your own understanding. (Proverbs 3:5)

**Materials Needed:**
- Three cups or small containers
- Warm and cold water

## Bible Lesson

Think about one of the unwise decisions you have made in the past. We all have such embarrassing moments when we must admit that we were wrong. Our own understanding of any circumstance is imperfect and always subject to error. To trust in the Lord means to not think too highly of oneself. In contrast, God's ways may sometimes seem incomprehensible to us, but he is always trustworthy.

God has blessed modern mankind with much knowledge. We have walked on the moon, explored the ocean depths, and split atoms. In the arts, great books and musical pieces have been written. In spite of this progress, however, there is much unhappiness in today's world. Crime, conflict, and tragedy remain with us nearly every day. Clearly, mankind's understanding and control of the world is very limited. But thankfully, God understands us better than we do ourselves. We need to call on him for direction in this life and for the eternal life to come.

## Science Activity

Each of our five senses—sight, hearing, taste, smell, and touch—is very useful in exploring the world. We depend on them continually for our knowledge and safety. However, these senses can occasionally mislead us. Our lesson activity shows how our sense of touch can be confused.

Three cups are filled with tap water. The first should be quite warm, although not uncomfortably hot to the touch. The second is at room temperature. The third cup contains cold water, perhaps with an ice cube added. Now place your left index finger in the warm water and your right index finger in the cold. Hold them there for about twenty seconds, perhaps while slowly counting to twenty. After this, quickly dip both fingers into the room-temperature water. The left index finger now will feel like it is submerged in cool water, while the right finger senses that it is in warm water. Yet they are both in the same container. The prior experience of the fingers causes them to falsely sense the normal water temperature. If you didn't know better, you would believe that your fingers were in entirely different containers.

An alternative approach is to blindfold a person initially. Guide them in moving their fingers from the hot and cold containers to the room-temperature water. They will be surprised when shown that their fingers are now in the same container.

The obvious lesson is that our senses cannot always be trusted. The sense of touch is valuable, especially when guarding against dangerous

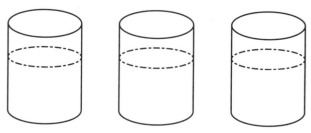

Three containers are filled with water—one warm, one room-temperature, and one with cold. They are used to confuse our sense of touch.

temperatures and burns, but it can be easily fooled. Likewise our own understanding of life and events can be wrong. We need direction from God's Word to make the right decisions.

## Science Explanation

The temperature of an object is a measure of the average motion or kinetic energy of the object's molecules. The more rapidly the molecules move or vibrate, the higher the temperature. Our molecules of skin tissue vibrate thousands of times each second, as if connected with tiny springs. The finger placed in the warm water absorbs some of the heat, which results in a still higher vibration of skin molecules. In the cold water, molecular motion within the finger is slowed. When both fingers are shifted to the water at room temperature, vibrational motion from the warmed finger is given up to the surrounding water. The warmed finger thus loses this energy and feels cool. Meanwhile, the finger from the ice water absorbs vibrational energy from room-temperature water and feels warmed as a result. Following the experiment, your sense of touch will soon return to normal.

# A Straight Path

**Theme:** With the Lord's help we can have purpose and direction in life.

**Bible Verse:** In all your ways acknowledge Him, and He shall direct your paths. (Proverbs 3:6)

**Materials Needed:**
- Sheets of newspaper
- Several volunteers

## Bible Lesson

People on the Lord's side have straight paths to follow. Not that this present life is perfect, but the Lord helps us continually to make choices and handle life's problems. In God's strength we can go forward with confidence that he leads us along. We talk to him in prayer and obey his Word, the Bible. In this way we will learn which paths to travel and which choices to make. In times of special need we can call upon his name for help. How sad to neglect the greatest resource available on earth.

## Science Activity

How about a paper-tearing contest? Give several people full sheets of newspaper. Tell one group to tear off narrow strips from top to bottom, perpendicular to the writing. The second group must tear the newspapers across the page, parallel to the printed lines. The contest is to see which group produces the neatest, straightest strips. It will soon be apparent that the second group has great difficulty. Have fun coaching this group, encouraging them to do better.

Newspapers generally tear much more easily down the page than across. A newspaper has internal wood fibers that are lined up in the direction in which the paper was rolled during manufacturing. These cellulose fibers are somewhat like invisible threads within the paper. The paper tears easily and relatively straight along this aligned direction. Against this grain, however, it is almost impossible to tear a straight line for any length. Those on the Lord's side have direction and purpose, like the straight strips of paper. Those who ignore the Lord, however, are headed for trouble and frustration, just like trying to evenly tear paper the hard way—against its internal grain.

Practice this newspaper tearing activity ahead of time. Some newspaper may tear the opposite way described, depending on the paper-making process.

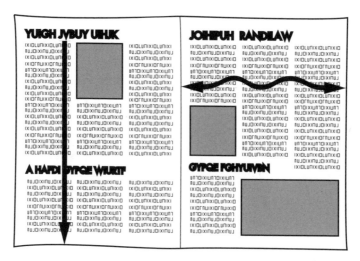

Most newspapers will tear straight in a downward direction (left) but unevenly across the page (right).

## Science Explanation

Papermaking techniques go back nearly two thousand years. Wood material is typically ground up and reduced to a slurry of loose fibers. This pulp then receives additives such as glue, clay, and color pigments. These additives determine the type and quality of the paper.

The liquid pulp is spread onto a conveyer belt. It is then pressed flat, dried, and smoothed. In this process the internal fibers tend to align themselves in the direction of the paper's movement. For this reason a newspaper usually has a preferred direction of tearing. Individual wood fibers can often be seen within the newspaper sheet, especially if it is held up to light.

The manufacture of notebook paper or stationery involves a finer grinding of wood fibers and additional filler materials. These types of paper will tear equally well in any direction.

# No Air to Breathe

**Theme:** God's gift of salvation, not our works, opens the way to heaven for us.

**Bible Verse:** There is a way that seems right to a man, but its end is the way of death. (Proverbs 14:12)

**Materials Needed:**
- Empty aquarium or large bowl
- Baking soda
- Vinegar
- Candle and match

## Bible Lesson

Early on the morning of August 21, 1986, the people living near Lake Nios in Cameroon, West Africa, went about their chores. Cattle grazed on the hillsides while children played games. Suddenly, a vast cloud of invisible gas bubbled up from the lake bottom like an enormous fountain and spread outward across the land. The carbon dioxide gas had no taste or smell, but it was deadly. Wherever it flowed, animals and entire families quickly suffocated. In just minutes, 1,750 people and many thousands of cattle were killed without warning. The air, which appeared to be normal and healthy, had become poisonous. Scientists do not fully understand why the lake underwent this tragic and sudden change, nor can they predict when it may happen again.

The Scripture verse reminds us that we can be sadly mistaken about the important things in life. For example, people have many different ideas about salvation and gaining a home in heaven:

Some get baptized and attend church without fail.

Some hope their good deeds will outweigh the bad.

Some give gifts to church or charity to "pay their way."

Some repeat special words or phrases thousands of times.

None of these methods is sufficient! As hard as one may try, it is simply impossible to *earn* a ticket to heaven. Motives and deeds may seem good enough, but by themselves they fall short. The morning air appeared pleasant to the people around Lake Nios, but it actually was deadly.

The Bible makes it clear that salvation is a gift given to those who place their faith in Christ (Ephesians 2:8–9). Good deeds are fine but are not sufficient to gain eternal life. Christ has already paid the price for us—take him at his word!

## Science Activity

This activity produces invisible carbon dioxide gas in the aquarium or other large, deep container. Add baking soda and vinegar to the tank, about ½ cup of each. The mixture will bubble and foam at the bottom. Carbon dioxide is heavier than air and will remain in the tank for several minutes.

Now light a candle in front of the group. Slowly lower it into the tank and the fire should quickly go out; carbon dioxide will not support a flame. If this doesn't work well, increase the amounts of baking soda and vinegar to make more carbon dioxide. Explain to the group that the air in the tank looks clear and breathable, but it actually suffocates the candle. Likewise, as our verse clearly states, some people's choices on the path to heaven may look good, but they actually cause spiritual suffocation.

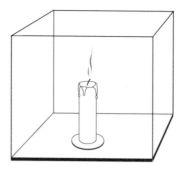

An aquarium containing vinegar mixed with baking soda shows the suffocating properties of carbon dioxide gas.

## Science Explanation

Baking soda is sodium bicarbonate, $NaHCO_3$. Vinegar is dilute acetic acid, $HC_2H_3O_2$. Their reaction together can be written as:

$$NaHCO_3 + HC_2H_3O_2 \rightarrow CO_2 + H_2O + NaC_2H_3O_2$$

The bubbling gas is carbon dioxide, $CO_2$. This gas is heavier than most other gases in the air. Here is a comparison table of the four most abundant gases in our atmosphere:

| Gas | Relative Weight | Percent Abundance in Air |
|---|---|---|
| Argon, Ar | 10 | 0.93 |
| Nitrogen, $N_2$ | 14 | 78.0 |
| Oxygen, $O_2$ | 32 | 21.0 |
| Carbon dioxide, $CO_2$ | 38 | 0.03 |

The carbon dioxide will not remain permanently in the container because gases slowly diffuse or spread outward into the surrounding air. The small amount of carbon dioxide produced is not dangerous. After all, we exhale carbon dioxide continually.

For further exploration, blow soap bubbles and let them fall into the aquarium. They contain some nitrogen gas and should float on the invisible carbon dioxide layer, suspended midway in the tank. As an alternative to vinegar and baking soda, Alka Seltzer and water can also be used to release carbon dioxide.

# Turning Away Anger

**Theme:** We can control the outcome of arguments if we have self-control.

**Bible Verse:** A soft answer turns away wrath, but a harsh word stirs up anger. (Proverbs 15:1)

**Materials Needed:**
- Large piece of cloth (e.g., sheet, towel, tablecloth)
- Egg
- Three volunteers

## Bible Lesson

People have a natural desire to answer harsh words with more of the same: "He can't get away with saying that, especially when I am right and he is wrong!" However, such heated arguments will only increase the problem instead of solving it. The proverb in this lesson gives a better approach: disarm your opponent by controlling your own emotions. There is no more effective strategy than listening to the other side of the issue and honestly trying to understand it. A gentle answer might include an apology or just a willingness to listen.

This approach certainly reflects a Christlike spirit and is a positive testimony to others.

## Science Activity

In this activity someone forcefully tosses a fresh egg at close range at a vertically suspended cloth held up by two brave volunteers. The bottom of the cloth is folded up to form a pocket, held in place by the volunteers. When the egg hits the loosely held cloth, there is enough "give" to safely slow down the egg without breaking it. The egg then slides harmlessly down the cloth and into the pocket below.

The egg could now be dropped onto a hard surface and broken to show that it is delicate and raw. The extended lesson is that a mishandled egg, like uncontrolled anger, has damaging results.

## Science Explanation

The technique with the cloth is similar to playing catch with bare hands. As you catch the ball, you can move your hands with the ball as

A suspended cloth sheet with a pocket formed at the bottom will safely catch a tossed egg.

you receive it to spread out the impact time and lessen the sting of the catch. The longer the stopping time, the smaller the resulting force. Likewise, the sheet slows down the moving egg in a way that protects it from breaking.

This slowing technique is the opposite of batting a ball. When a bat connects with a ball, the ball experiences a large force. As home run hitters know, one secret of success is a fast swing.

According to Newton's second law of motion, the force needed to stop a moving object directly depends on how quickly the object is stopped. If an object strikes a hard surface, it may stop instantly and experience an enormous force. If the object can be decelerated more slowly, however, the force needed to stop it is greatly reduced.

Automobiles are designed with Newton's second law of motion in view. The bumpers are designed to give in a collision, lengthening the impact time and also absorbing the blow. A car's steering wheel and dashboard are also padded to lengthen impact time and thus soften bumps to the head. In an emergency, an airbag likewise protects a person during sudden deceleration.

Isaac Newton studied motion three centuries ago. He probably would have preferred that his conclusions be called God's laws rather than Newton's laws. He strongly believed that the Creator had established the rules of the physical world.

# Haste Makes Waste

**Theme:** It pays to be patient.

**Bible Verse:** The discretion of a man makes him slow to anger, and his glory is to overlook a transgression. (Proverbs 19:11)

**Materials Needed:**
- Wooden paint-stirring stick or thin scrap of wood
- Sheets of newspaper

## Bible Lesson

Patience can be shown several ways. It includes an understanding attitude, a listening ear, wise counsel, and forgiveness for others. King Solomon reminds us in Proverbs 19:11 that patience is a sign of wisdom and maturity. Even in Old Testament times, patience was often lacking among people. And on our modern highways especially, violent arguments called "road rage" sometimes arise over trivial incidents and delays. Such people completely lose control of their own emotions and behavior. How sad it is to fill our few days on earth with unnecessary anger and impatience. Such emotions are unhealthy for both the body and the mind.

Let us look to the Lord as our example for patience. Ever since the biblical fall and its curse due to man's disobedience, this world has dishonored God in many ways. Still, God patiently waits for us to be drawn to him. He is willing to forgive our offenses far more than we could ever forgive one another. By showing patience toward others, we can reflect God's love to those around us.

## Science Activity

This activity will illustrate the ruin that can result from haste. Place a thin board or stick on a tabletop with nearly half the stick length extending out over the edge. A wooden paint stirrer or similar stick works well. Now place two sheets of newspaper over the stick and smooth them flat. A single newspaper sheet will sometimes tear, so two are recommended.

The idea is to push downward on the protruding stick as a lever, thereby raising the newspaper. Show the group that a slow push easily pivots the stick and lifts much of the newspaper upward as expected. Now ask what will happen if the same task is done quickly, by striking the stick. The usual guess is that the newspaper will rapidly fly upward or perhaps tear itself in half. However, this is not the case. The strongest blow should not budge the newspaper. Instead, the paper will remain flat and the stick will usually break into two pieces. Stand to one side, and take care that the broken stick does not fly through the

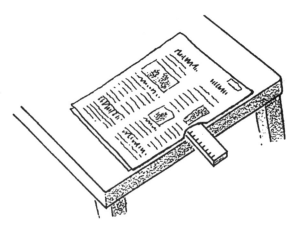

The newspaper refuses to move, breaking the stick when it is struck downward.

air toward anyone. Practice ahead of time with extra sticks. Make the concluding point that a slow, patient movement easily lifts the paper. Likewise a patient approach is often the best way to solve problems. Haste makes waste, as illustrated by the broken stick!

## Science Explanation

This type of activity is sometimes called a *discrepant event*. That is, the results are contrary to one's intuition. It seems almost impossible that lightweight newspaper sheets can withstand the sudden upward force from a wooden stick. Actually, air pressure is involved in breaking the stick. If the covered stick is raised slowly, the paper offers little resistance. Air easily moves inward beneath the paper, and the pressure above and beneath the paper surfaces remains equal. With rapid motion, however, a temporary thin layer of partial vacuum occurs beneath the rising newspaper. This results in less air pressure under the newspaper than on its upper surface.

Air pressure at the earth's surface averages 14.7 pounds per square inch (psi). In striking the stick, suppose there results an upper/lower pressure difference of just 1 psi. Also, suppose that the central part of the newspaper comprises about 100 square inches (10 inches by 10 inches). There results an unbalanced downward force of 100 pounds holding the newspaper down, and the stick therefore quickly breaks. The actual total weight on the entire top of a flat newspaper due to air pressure may be as great as 4,000 pounds, or 2 tons.

Air pressure results from the weight of the earth's atmosphere. Living on the earth beneath this "ocean" of air, we don't often notice its resulting air pressure. This activity is one of many dramatic ways to illustrate the air pressure that surrounds us at all times.

# Watch Your Temper

**Theme:** An uncontrolled temper is foolish and also dishonors the Lord.

**Bible Verse:** A man of great wrath will suffer punishment; for if you rescue him, you will have to do it again. (Proverbs 19:19)

**Materials Needed:**
- Small container with a press-on lid, not a screw-on top
  * (a small Tupperware container with lid works well)
- Vinegar
- Baking soda

## Bible Lesson

An uncontrolled temper often leads to improper words and actions. The results may include unwise decisions and broken friendships. Whatever the eventual penalty, it is usually worse than the initial problem that caused the temper tantrum in the first place. Sadly, as the Bible verse explains, a hot-tempered person does not easily learn patience. Instead, he repeats the same error again and again.

We all have seen examples of a hotheaded person, many of them humorous. He kicks his lawn mower when it won't start, hurting his foot; he breaks his golf club over his knee after a bad putt; she slams the door and a picture on the wall shatters. Actually, there is a more serious side to losing one's temper, especially for the Christian. The habit reveals a loss of self-control and discipline. Instead of letting the Spirit of Christ lead, the person allows the sinful nature to take over. Losing one's temper is definitely not a good testimony.

The cure to the temper problem is found in Proverbs 15:1—"A soft answer turns away wrath, but a harsh word stirs up anger." A soft or gentle answer is the exact opposite of a temper outburst. It leaves no room for uncontrolled anger if it is sincere. For further discussion of temper, see lesson 34, which is based on Proverbs 15:1.

## Science Activity

Uncontrolled temper will be illustrated by the pressure built up inside a plastic container. For the activity, put 2 tablespoons of baking soda into the container along with ½ cup of vinegar and quickly press the top on. To delay the reaction, the baking soda can be wrapped up in small pieces of tissue. As the paper moistens, bubbling will start. The chemical reaction between vinegar and baking soda produces carbon dioxide gas. If the reaction is sluggish, shake the container slightly. (An alternative to the vinegar and baking soda reaction is to put water in the container and drop in pieces of Alka Seltzer tablets.)

After the pressure builds up sufficiently, the cover will pop off. Have a towel handy to catch the foam that often overflows from the container.

Vinegar and baking soda sealed in a small container produce carbon dioxide gas. The resulting pressure will "pop the top."

## Science Explanation

The chemicals involved in this activity are vinegar (a dilute solution of acetic acid, $CH_3CO_2H$), baking soda (sodium bicarbonate, $NaHCO_3$), and carbon dioxide gas ($CO_2$). Carbon dioxide forms in large amounts when vinegar and baking soda are combined. This harmless gas is also in carbonated drinks to give them their fizz. When a container of soda is thoroughly shaken and then opened, it gives an effect similar to that of this lesson's activity.

# Dancing Raisins

**Theme:** Seek the Lord's direction.

**Bible Verse:** The plans of the diligent lead to profit as surely as haste leads to poverty. (Proverbs 21:5 NIV)

**Materials Needed:**
- One dozen raisins
- Clear drinking glass
- Large bottle of clear soda

## Bible Lesson

We live in a world of rapid movement. Airports and highways are crowded; information surges through electronic networks and the air. We often feel the stress from this busy lifestyle. We must make quick decisions, then suffer the consequences if things go wrong.

In the book of Proverbs, King Solomon cautions us regarding hasty decisions. Whenever possible, we should exercise the ability God has given us to think through to the results of our actions. It takes extra effort to consider the consequences, but this effort is very worthwhile. Many potential problems can be avoided in this way. For example, major purchases should be preceded by considering their impact on our budget. We must also remember that a quality purchase is often wiser than a substandard bargain.

Notice that Solomon's proverb refers to material gain. This is certainly not the chief goal in life, but profit rather than poverty can enable us to help others and also to avoid financial tensions. Not all problems or opportunities that come our way can be anticipated. However, many can, and people who plan ahead will enjoy a calmer life as a result.

## Science Activity

Years ago this activity commonly involved dropping mothballs into water. As the mothballs dissolve, carbon dioxide bubbles form on their surfaces and float them to the top. There the bubbles break loose and the mothballs sink back to the bottom. The restless up and down motion of the mothballs humorously illustrates our modern lifestyles.

The activity can be done more simply by dropping raisins into a glass of clear soda. The raisins gather carbon dioxide at the bottom, float to the top and lose their bubbles, then drop downward again. This works best if one uses fresh, dark raisins and room-temperature soda. Raisins are not essential; peanuts, buttons, uncooked spaghetti, or other small objects will also gather bubbles and float momentarily. While watching the "dancing raisins," ask the participants if their schedules sometimes are similar: much running around with little real progress being made. Ask for suggestions on how we can

Dancing raisins rise and fall in a solution containing carbon dioxide gas.

prevent hasty mistakes, unproductive errands, and wasted time. The list might include:

Asking God for direction through prayer.

Seeking counsel from others.

Combining several errands into one trip.

Taking adequate time for reflection before making major decisions.

## Science Explanation

Soft drinks hold a considerable amount of dissolved carbon dioxide, $CO_2$. This results in dilute carbonic acid, which gives soda its familiar tangy taste. At warmer temperatures the soda can hold less gas so it bubbles upward. You have probably seen the result of a rapid loss of carbon dioxide when a soda container is vigorously shaken before opening. As an alternative to soda, Alka Seltzer and water also release carbon dioxide.

The raisins or other small objects have a density just slightly greater than water. If small bubbles of $CO_2$ attach to them, they are buoyed upward to the surface. They will remain there until the bubbles separate; then they drop downward again.

# Splash!

**Theme:** Those who trust in the Lord are secure.

**Bible Verse:** The fear of man brings a snare, but whoever trusts in the Lord shall be safe. (Proverbs 29:25)

**Materials Needed:**
- Bucket
- Water

## Bible Lesson

Christians are not immune to worry and doubt in this uncertain world. They do not have to face the problems of life in their own strength, however. Their lives are built on a strong foundation that cannot be shaken. Whatever happens, believers know that the Lord is present from the beginning to the end. Remembering the Lord's strength during times of trial will result in two benefits. First, Christians can testify to others of God's grace. Second, this can be a time of spiritual growth. Life may be difficult at times, but it is also exciting to see how the Lord helps believers through tough situations. Their success lies in knowing that God is in control.

## Science Activity

This is an activity that many of us did as youngsters. The trick is to twirl a bucket of water in a vertical circle without spilling. If the bucket is moved faster than a certain minimum speed (about 10 feet per second), the water cannot possibly spill out. At the top of the arc when the bucket is upside down, the downward gravity force simply causes the water to move in the circle rather than to spill downward.

Begin by showing everyone an empty bucket. It should have a secure handle that cannot come loose. Then pour about a quart of water into the bucket to show there is no trick. The amount of water does not matter; it does not affect the necessary bucket speed. After you pour water from a jar, you could also drop the jar into the bucket, just for good measure. Begin the circling motion with a few back-and-forth swings at the bottom of the arc. You will automatically feel how fast the bucket must move to safely revolve in a complete circle. You can then minimize the speed, slowing the bucket to the point where the water becomes slightly unstable at the top of the circle. This is also a good activity for a volunteer to perform. Make sure that there is adequate clearance on all sides for swinging.

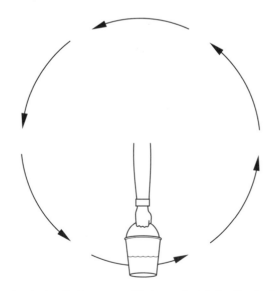

Water in a bucket that is swung swiftly in a vertical circle will not spill out.

This busy life sometimes seems to whirl like the bucket, and we wonder if we have lost control. However, just as the water cannot escape the bucket, the Christian is entirely secure in the arms of the Lord.

## Science Explanation

Circular motion is common in nature. Consider, for example, the moon's orbit around the earth. Like the spinning bucket, the moon circles the earth with a constant speed of over 2,000 miles per hour. And yet there is no danger of the moon escaping into the cold depths of space or crashing into the earth. Instead, the moon remains within the firm grasp of the earth's gravity force.

Circular motion always requires an inward pull. This is called the *centripetal* force, which means "toward the center" of the circle. It may be gravity, a string pulling inward on a ball, or a strong arm holding a bucket.

God's strength may be invisible like gravity, but it is likewise dependable. After all, it is God who established gravity and the rules for circular motion.

# Water beneath Our Feet

**Theme:** God supplies our daily needs.

**Bible Verse:** All the rivers run into the sea, yet the sea is not full; to the place from which the rivers come, there they return again. (Ecclesiastes 1:7)

**Materials Needed:**
- About 30 marbles
- Clear glass or transparent cup
- Measuring cup
- Water

## Bible Lesson

Our lives depend on a continuous supply of fresh water. Think about the last time the water was temporarily turned off in your home. At such times it is surprising how often one automatically reaches for a faucet—with no result. Without water, normal routines quickly come to a halt.

Many people around the world obtain their water from underground. Rain and melted snow soak into the soil, where they continue to move downward and are slowly filtered by sand and gravel.

143

The resulting water then accumulates within underground layers of rock and gravel, sometimes called aquifers. This water can later be brought to the surface with a pump or open well. Groundwater is available almost everywhere on earth at varying depths. The upper water surface, called the water table, may be only tens of feet deep, or it may be hundreds of feet deep in desert locations.

Our verse describes an apparent mystery involving streams and rivers. How can they keep flowing day after day, even during times of drought? The answer is that water is continually recycled. Water enters streams along their length through underground springs and seepage. Groundwater is constantly on the move, gradually flowing downward by the influence of gravity toward streambeds, lakes, and seas.

Solomon in his wisdom recognized the movement of the earth's water. Evaporation occurs from seas, lakes, and also from the land. Much of this moisture later returns to the earth as precipitation of rain and snow. In this way sea level remains constant, the land is refreshed and watered, and groundwater reserves are recharged. This movement of water, called the water cycle or *hydrologic* cycle, is a precious and essential gift from the Creator.

## Science Activity

We will explore the amount of water that is stored underground. Teams of two or three people can do the activity. A measuring cup is filled to a convenient level with marbles, perhaps 1 to 2 cups total. It doesn't matter if the marbles are of unequal sizes or if a few extend slightly above the selected measuring line.

Now transfer the measured quantity of marbles to the clear container and fill the measuring cup with water. Pour this water onto the marbles until the liquid level reaches the top of the marbles. Water now fills the openings between the marbles, just as it fills small spaces underground. The marbles represent buried sand or gravel. A look at the water remaining in the measuring cup will show how much water has been poured out.

Participants will find that the spaces between the marbles hold a surprisingly large amount of water. If there was originally an amount of marbles equal to 1 cup, then the water added should be nearly ½ cup. This activity helps to illustrate how trillions of gallons of water can be stored underground between small pebbles and sand grains.

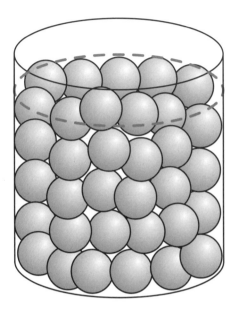

A container filled with marbles, sand, or gravel has considerable additional space available for water.

## Science Explanation

The amount of water that can be held by underground materials is called the *porosity*. It is defined as the percentage of the total volume of underground rock or sediment that consists of open pore space. For example, if 0.4 cups of water can be added to 1 cup of marbles, then the porosity is

$$\frac{0.4}{1} (100\%) = 40\%$$

That is, there is 40 percent open space, now filled with water. The following table gives porosity ranges for several common underground materials.

| Material | Porosity (percent) |
| --- | --- |
| Soil | 35–50 |
| Clay | 35–80 |

| Material | Porosity (percent) |
|---|---|
| Sand | 30–50 |
| Gravel | 25–40 |
| Limestone | 0–20 |
| Sandstone | 0–30 |
| Volcanic rock | 0–50 |

It can be seen that most materials hold considerable amounts of water. To extend this activity, the marbles can be replaced by sand or gravel. The resulting porosity values can then be compared with those in the list.

# Whiter than Snow

**Theme:** God's forgiveness is complete.

**Bible Verse:** "Come now, and let us reason together," says the Lord, "though your sins are like scarlet, they shall be as white as snow; though they are red like crimson, they shall be as wool." (Isaiah 1:18)

**Materials Needed:**
- Large jar with cover
- Strips of colored construction paper
- Liquid bleach

## Bible Lesson

Christopher was a mess when he finally arrived home from school. Earlier it had looked like a good day for bicycling. By afternoon, however, a light rain was falling. The bike ride home started out okay, just a few raindrops, which felt good on his skin. Soon, however, Christopher was having difficulty dodging the puddles. A wide streak of brown mud from the rear wheel began forming up the back of his white jacket and even in his hair. As many others have found out, it is hazardous to ride a bicycle in the rain!

Finally Christopher was within sight of home, with the mud now dribbling down his forehead. He made quite a sight as he stood dripping inside the kitchen door. The opposite of a white snowman, Christopher now was covered with dirt. Instead of being upset, Mom couldn't help but laugh at the sight, and Christopher did the same. Into the shower he went while his dirty clothes were taken directly to the laundry room. Very soon Christopher was clean again and wearing dry clothes. Even his jacket was white again.

Christopher thanked his mom for rescuing him. Together they remembered their breakfast devotion about the Lord washing away sins and making lives as white as snow in his sight. In fact, the Bible said that God no longer *remembered* the sins of his children (Jeremiah 31:34; Hebrews 8:12). "Okay, Mom," Christopher said, "how soon will you forget this muddy afternoon?"

## Science Activity

Carefully pour about ½ to 1 inch of liquid bleach into a large, wide-mouthed jar. Stand the colored strips of paper inside the jar so they are partially submerged. Put the cover on the jar to avoid fumes.

It should take just minutes to bleach the strips to a white color. If some color remains, you can stress that only God does a perfect job

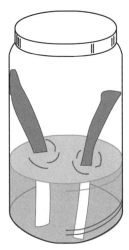

Strips of construction paper are bleached white.

of removing stains. Have some of the original paper available nearby to show the contrast in colors. The comparison is quite impressive and will help lock in the "white as snow" concept of forgiveness.

## Science Explanation

There are several forms of bleach, one of the most common being a solution of sodium chlorite, $NaClO_2$. The bleaching activity is largely due to chlorine dioxide, $ClO_2$. The chlorine oxidizes many colored substances to colorless compounds. Large amounts of chlorine are used commercially in bleaching wood pulp for paper and also in making cotton cloth. Typical sources of chlorine are brine wells, salt mines, and ocean water.

One can also bleach flowers in the jar, and surprising colors may result. The chemical reaction with bleach breaks down certain colors and not others. Red, pink, and purple flowers may turn green due to chlorophyll that was masked by the other colors. In contrast, yellow flowers usually show little color change with bleach.

# A Blind Spot

**Theme:** New life in Christ opens our spiritual eyes.

**Bible Verse:** Then the eyes of the blind shall be opened, and the ears of the deaf shall be unstopped. (Isaiah 35:5)

**Materials Needed:**
- Paper
- Pencils or pens

## Bible Lesson

Isaiah 35 is a beautiful picture of Israel's future from the prophet Isaiah's vantage point around 700 BC. The good news is best enjoyed when compared with the dire judgment of chapter 34. The eyesight and hearing described in our key verse picture the gift of salvation. In knowing God, our eyes and ears are opened to things we simply couldn't see before:

God's love for us

The value of God's Word

Answers to prayer

God's leading in our life

The glories of creation

The verse also had a literal fulfillment when Christ walked among mankind many generations ago. At that time he physically healed the eyes and ears of needy people. Surely Christ had Isaiah 35 in mind when he sent a message of hope to John the Baptist (Luke 7:19–23). What a Savior we have: one who can heal eye and ear problems, both physical and spiritual.

This activity reminds us of the complexity of our eyes. We all have a blind spot, though, and can miss seeing things. Likewise, the person who does not know God is blind to the greatest gifts in life. New life in Christ opens our eyes to these gifts from above.

## Science Activity

Participants need a piece of paper and a pen or pencil. Each person is asked to draw an X and O as dark as possible about 2½ inches apart and ½ inch high with the X on the left.

Now hold the paper at arm's length. Look at the X with your right eye while closing or covering your left eye. The O should still be seen far off to the right side. Very slowly bring the paper closer to your eye. At about 8 inches distance, you should notice that the O completely disappears from the page. The paper is now located at your blind spot. Nearer or farther away, the O will reappear. Any

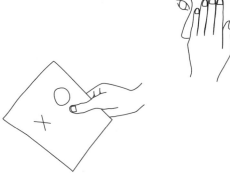

As a paper with two letters on it is moved closer to your eye, you notice a blind spot when one letter disappears.

marks on the paper will suffice; the X and O are simply convenient symbols to see.

Try reversing the experiment, covering the right eye and looking at the O with the left eye while moving the paper. The same effect will result, this time with the X disappearing from view.

## Science Explanation

Light passes through the eye's cornea and lens, focusing on the retina on the back surface of the eyeball. This retina is filled with millions of light sensors called rods and cones. There is one spot on the retina, however, where the optic nerve connects the eye to the brain. Sensors are lacking in this small region. When light focuses on this blind spot, an image cannot be seen. Most often this is not noticeable since one eye compensates for the other. When one eye is covered, however, as in this activity, the blind spot becomes apparent. The optic nerve connection, or blind spot, is actually located off center on the retina, so visual problems are usually avoided, even with just one eye. The Creator thought of everything!

# Floating on Air

**Theme:** The Lord provides "wind beneath our wings," giving us support.

**Bible Verse:** But those who wait on the LORD shall renew their strength; they shall mount up with wings like eagles, they shall run and not be weary, they shall walk and not faint. (Isaiah 40:31)

**Materials Needed:**
- Hair dryer
- Balloon, ping-pong ball, or other lightweight ball

## Bible Lesson

To hope in the Lord, or to wait upon the Lord, does not mean to give up or to sit back and do nothing. Instead, it means not giving in to the pressures and temptations of life. It is trusting steadily in God, fully expecting him to make things right in the end.

Eagles can fly with no apparent effort. They will soar for hours on thermals, rising currents of warm air. Likewise, Christians have invisible support from on high. This is not to say that we will never get sick or experience failure. The promise is that God will be with us during the high times of soaring and also during the low times of testing. The promise involves exchanging a reliance on our own limited strength for complete trust in Christ. Lasting strength, freedom, and endurance come only from God.

## Science Activity

Perhaps you have seen this activity in a store window as an eye-catcher. A ball is suspended permanently in the air by a vacuum hose. It jumps and bounces around but does not fall. In science this is called the Bernoulli effect, whereby the ball is supported by the stream of moving air. The air pressure is actually smaller within the airstream than it is around the outside. The greater outside pressure pushes inward on the ball from all sides, thus suspending it in the moving air. Whenever the ball begins to leave the airstream, higher pressure pushes it back into the center.

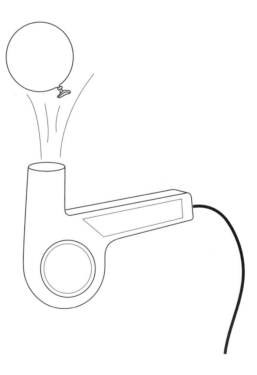

A balloon or lightweight ball placed in the airstream of a hair dryer will float in the air.

The electric hair dryer must have a good speed of air, which need not be heated. Hold the dryer steady or fasten it to a support. A balloon, light ball, some cotton, or even a paper wad can be supported by the upward airflow. A vacuum cleaner also works well, but only if the airflow can be reversed from suction to an outward airflow.

Objects will remain suspended as long as the invisible airstream is active. Stop the airflow by covering the source with your hand and the object will fall. In the same way, an eagle would fall from the sky if it lost its supporting air. For the believer, there is no such danger of a power failure.

## Science Explanation

The change in pressure caused by moving air can be substantial. For example, an airplane wing is designed to cause greater air speed above the wing surface than below. This results in higher pressure beneath the wing than above. The many thousands of pounds of upward lift cause the plane to fly. Winged flight is not possible on the moon or in space, where there is no air and therefore no pressure differences.

Daniel Bernoulli expressed the speed-pressure principle in 1738: "The pressure of a fluid decreases with increased velocity of the fluid." This Bernoulli effect is also responsible for such details as the curving of a baseball and the motion of a Frisbee.

# Wonderful Water

**Theme:** God's showers of blessing include his creative design of water.

**Bible Verse:** I will make them and the places all around My hill a blessing; and I will cause showers to come down in their season; there shall be showers of blessing. (Ezekiel 34:26)

**Materials Needed:**
- Two thermometers
- Paper towel
- Water
- Electric fan

## Bible Lesson

Ezekiel 34:25–31 describes a future time when God will heal the land and care for his people. This will include showers of blessing, the title of a well-known hymn written by Daniel Whittle a century ago:

> There shall be showers of blessing,
> This is the promise of love;
> There shall be seasons refreshing,
> Sent from the Savior above.

Rain showers provide many benefits for the earth: cleansing of dust and chemicals from the air, watering of plants, recharging of groundwater aquifers, and filling of ponds and reservoirs. Without rain, the earth would soon become a difficult place for life to exist. In our exploration of space, we have found no other planet with rain showers, or any liquid water at all. There is no place like home! The passage in Ezekiel reminds us that God's blessings are like refreshing rain. In fact, his blessings are much more precious than rain because they never end.

## Science Activity

This activity shows that the evaporation of water is a cooling process. You will need two thermometers, the kind with small bulbs at the bottom. They should be easy to read and identical, or at least similar.

Thoroughly wet a small piece of paper towel with room temperature water and wrap it loosely around the bottom bulb of one thermometer. Hold the thermometers side by side and show the group that both give the same degree reading. Now turn on the fan and place both

Wet and dry thermometers give different readings in a breeze.

thermometers in the breeze. The plain thermometer will not change its reading substantially. As for the thermometer with the wet paper towel at its base, the temperature should drop as much as six to ten degrees within two to three minutes.

This experiment shows how our bodies are cooled by the evaporation of perspiration. The process removes many heat *calories* from our skin, regulating our body temperature. Without this ability, hot weather would bring much greater danger of sunstroke or heat exhaustion. When the humidity is high, skin evaporation is hindered and one feels uncomfortable. Humidity is actually a greater factor than the temperature in determining our comfort level.

## Science Explanation

Evaporation is a wonderfully complex process. Water consists of vibrating, moving molecules. Collisions between these molecules within the liquid can cause some of them to leave the surface and move into the air. They become water vapor or humidity.

The average speed of water molecules is a measure of the water temperature. When the faster molecules escape by evaporation, the temperature of the remaining water molecules therefore drops. This is exactly what we observe with the thermometers. The breeze causes faster water molecules to escape from the wet paper towel, cooling it and also cooling the thermometer. Meanwhile, the dry thermometer changes little. A weather forecaster compares wet and dry thermometers in a similar way with a device called a psychrometer. The humidity of the air can be accurately measured in this way. Low humidity is indicated by a large difference between the wet and dry bulb readings.

In dry climates, swamp coolers operate on this principle. They evaporate water and circulate the resulting cool air around the room. Also, you may notice this cooling effect when alcohol is rubbed on your skin by a nurse before an injection. The alcohol evaporates very quickly, removing calories of heat from your skin in the process.

If we could only see the trillions of water molecules within a drop of water! They are rapidly moving about in a blur, with some ricocheting into the surrounding air. There is fascinating activity on the small, invisible scale of atoms and molecules.

# Walking Together

**Theme:** Friendship with Christ means walking in his ways.

**Bible Verse:** Can two walk together, unless they are agreed? (Amos 3:3)

**Materials Needed:**
- Fresh egg
- Hard-boiled egg

## Bible Lesson

It is a delight to take a relaxing walk with a friend. Ideas and encouragement can be easily shared in this setting. Walking with someone is beneficial for both mind and body. Sometimes, however, a friendship is sadly broken by disagreement. Then the friends can no longer walk together in peace, and both suffer as a result. Conflicts quickly remove the joy of walking and talking.

Our key verse refers to Israel's broken relationship with God. After their exodus from Egypt, the Jewish people soon turned away from the Lord. The Israelites still expected God's benefits and protection, but they no longer worshiped him. The prophet Amos told the Israelites that they could not expect God's presence and protection unless they returned to him. Over and over again in history, Israel turned away from the only one who could bless them.

The answer to the question of Amos 3:3 is a clear *no*. Both parties must be in agreement for harmony to result. God had not changed, but Israel had fallen away from fellowship. Amos was giving the people a wake-up call to their need for repentance.

Make sure that your friendship with others remains strong and positive. If there has been a breakdown in communication, make the first move toward restoration. Even more important, we must consider our relationship with God. Are we walking with him? If not, it is we ourselves who need to change.

## Science Activity

"Walking together" can be illustrated with two eggs, one hard-boiled and one fresh. Show the group how easily the hard-boiled egg spins on a table. Once spinning, the egg can be quickly stopped by placing your finger on it.

The fresh egg represents disagreeing friends who cannot walk together. Try spinning the fresh egg exactly like the hard-boiled one.

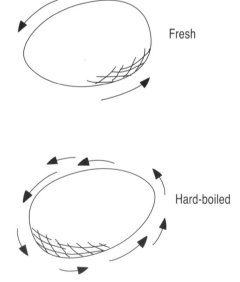

A hard-boiled egg spins and stops more easily than a fresh egg.

There is now a problem: the harder you try to spin a fresh egg, the less easily it turns. It resists the spinning motion. You can explain that the liquid materials inside the fresh egg are pulling against each other. Once the fresh egg is turning slowly, place your finger on top to stop the motion, then quickly let go. The fresh egg will start spinning again and continue turning slowly by itself.

Agreement with a friend is shown by the boiled egg, which readily spins and stops just as expected. It is entirely dependable. Disagreement is shown by the fresh egg; it behaves erratically and does not do what is expected. Let's be more like the boiled egg and behave like dependable friends.

## Science Explanation

The behavior of the two eggs follows from Isaac Newton's first law of motion, also called the law of inertia. The word *inertia* means "lazy" or "sluggish." The rule states that objects at rest remain at rest, and objects in motion remain in motion, unless they experience a changing force.

The boiled egg is solid; it spins easily and also stops quickly. The fresh egg, however, contains a yolk floating in the liquid egg white. In this egg, the yolk's inertia causes it to lag behind and resist the turning motion. When this egg is finally turning, stopping it does not completely halt the movement of the yolk within. The yolk bumps against the inside of the shell and causes the egg to turn again slowly. The parts of the fresh egg pull against each other and prevent a smooth turning motion.

# Rocks That Fizz

**Theme:** God outlasts the mountains.

**Bible Verse:** He stood and measured the earth; He looked and startled the nations. And the everlasting mountains were scattered, the perpetual hills bowed. His ways are everlasting. (Habakkuk 3:6)

**Materials Needed:**
- Vinegar
- Clear glass container
- Any combination of
  * chalk
  * small seashells
  * eggshells
  * limestone or cement fragments

## Bible Lesson

Mountains are usually considered to be ancient and permanent features. Their majesty is one of the greatest sights in all of creation. However, Habakkuk 3:6 gives a totally different perspective: compared with the Lord, even the mountains are insignificant and temporary.

The book of Habakkuk describes God's holiness and also his patience with a world that is evil. Our key verse pictures the conclusion of this present world system. The mountains are not exempt; they will quickly crumble and be scattered. Revelation 16:20 further states that someday the mountains and islands will disappear.

It is important to remember that all physical things on earth and in the sky above are temporary. Our bodies grow older and don't work as well. Houses creak and crack; machines break down. These processes have been going on ever since sin entered the world. Someday, perhaps soon, the Lord will return and make new heavens and a new earth. Only what is done for God has lasting value.

## Science Activity

This activity shows how hard, seemingly permanent objects can be dissolved away. Neither mountains nor rocks last forever. Pour one cup or more of vinegar into a clear glass container. The stronger the vinegar solution, the better. Vinegar is usually diluted to 4 to 10 percent acidity, according to the label. It may help to let a glass of vinegar sit open for several days. Water will evaporate away, leaving behind the stronger vinegar solution.

Drop several of the listed objects into the vinegar. The vinegar is a weak acid and will cause the objects to bubble and slowly dissolve.

Various common materials containing calcite will fizz and slowly dissolve in vinegar.

It may take only minutes, or it may take hours for some objects to noticeably dissolve. The listed objects, including limestone, are all composed of the mineral calcite. A small piece of limestone from outdoors is especially impressive to use since we usually think of rocks as indestructible. Limestone is quite common in most areas and is sometimes used as crushed stone for driveways. If chalk is placed in the vinegar, small pieces will soon break off and the chalk will eventually disappear. Comment to the observers that no physical objects on this earth are permanent.

## Science Explanation

The dissolving process is a speeded-up version of acid rain. Precipitation is somewhat acidic and reacts chemically with surfaces: car paint tarnishes, plant leaves become unhealthy, and tombstones slowly become unreadable. Vinegar is a diluted form of acetic acid, $HC_2H_3O_2$. The mineral calcite has the formula $CaCO_3$. When these chemicals come in contact, the gas that bubbles off is carbon dioxide, $CO_2$:

$$CaCO_3 + 2HC_2H_3O_2 \rightarrow H_2O + Ca + 2C_2H_3O_2 + CO_2$$

This reaction is regularly used by geologists as a test for detecting the mineral calcite in unknown rock samples. A small amount of acid is placed on the rock sample. If small bubbles appear, the unknown mineral is calcite.

# A Smothered Candle

**Theme:** The gospel must be shared.

**Bible Verse:** Nor do they light a lamp and put it under a basket, but on a lampstand, and it gives light to all who are in the house. (Matthew 5:15)

**Materials Needed:**
- Votive candle
- Lighter
- Large clear bottle or glass
- Shallow bowl
- Water
- Food coloring

## Bible Lesson

In our early Sunday school years we sing

> This little light of mine,
> I'm going to let it shine . . .
> Hide it under a bushel, no!

This light pictures our new life in Christ. If we truly comprehend what he has done for us, we will be compelled to share Christ with others. How can such exciting, life-changing news be kept under cover? The term *basket* in our key verse refers to a dry measure of volume, about one peck in Bible times, or one quarter the size of a modern bushel basket.

Matthew 5:16 goes on to acknowledge the good deeds that result from a Christ-centered life. The verse teaches that hiding one's Christian light either under a bushel or behind a closed door is selfish. After all, any praise that others give for our good deeds belongs to God, not to us.

## Science Activity

Place the lighted candle in the shallow container. It should be partially submerged in water. The depth of water is unimportant, as long as the glass will easily fit over the candle and down into the water. The candle burns brightly while in the open.

Next, put the glass in place over the candle and down into the water. Several interesting things will happen quickly. The candle will continue burning for a few seconds. It will also heat the air inside the glass, causing large gas bubbles to leave the bottom of the glass. Then the candle will go out as it exhausts its oxygen supply. The air remaining inside the glass then cools and contracts, pulling water back up into the glass. The rising water level is more easily seen if a small amount of food coloring has been added to the water.

The candle burns fine as long as it is in the open air. However, when sealed up inside the glass without oxygen, the flame cannot continue

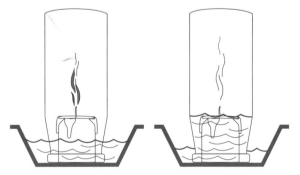

A candle trapped under a glass cannot continue burning.

burning. Likewise, the Christian life is not designed to be sealed up and kept a secret. The Good News is meant to be shared with others.

## Science Explanation

This experiment is often explained incorrectly. The burning candle is said to use up all the oxygen, resulting in a vacuum that pulls the water upward into the glass. This is incorrect. The oxygen gas is converted to an equal amount of carbon dioxide gas, not a vacuum. As the candle goes out from lack of oxygen, it is the cooling, contracting air which then causes a partial vacuum inside the glass. A simple combustion reaction can be written for the candle involving carbon, C, oxygen, $O_2$, and the resulting carbon dioxide, $CO_2$:

$$C + O_2 \rightarrow CO_2$$

When the air initially expands by heating, its volume change is proportional to the temperature increase. If the air inside the glass doubles in temperature, then a glassful of air escapes in the initial bubbling process. When the candle is extinguished, the remaining air likewise cools and contracts. It is quite surprising how high the water level rises inside the glass.

# A Quick Change

**Theme:** Now is the time to trust in the Lord; later may be too late.

**Bible Verses:** Then two men will be in the field: one will be taken and the other left. Two women will be grinding at the mill: one will be taken and the other left. (Matthew 24:40–41)

**Materials Needed:**
- Small glass or plastic containers
- Index cards, 3" x 5" or 4" x 6"
- Pennies

## Bible Lesson

In this day of self-sufficiency it is important to remember that the world is temporary and life is short. The Lord began this present world, and he will also end it someday. The Scripture lesson describes the second coming of Christ after the time of distress is past (Matthew 24:29). Two people working side by side will be separated, one taken away to judgment while the other is left to enjoy the Lord's presence. Verses 37–39 compare this separation to the great flood, when the wicked perished and the faithful remained safe on board the ark. The message still applies to us. We should always be prepared and ready for the Lord's coming.

## Science Activity

This activity is fun for all ages. It involves the rapid removal of a card from under a coin so that the coin falls into a glass. First, cover the top of the glass with the card and place the coin on the card. Next, knock the card from under the coin with a rapid flick of the finger. This takes a bit of practice. The goal is to get the penny to drop downward into the glass.

The coin is said to have inertia. The rapid motion of the card does not put appreciable force on the coin. Suddenly, the coin loses its support and gravity takes over. Similarly, life conditions at any moment can change quickly, especially when the Lord returns.

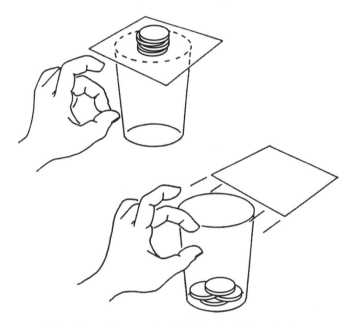

When the card is removed rapidly, the coins fall into the glass.

## Science Explanation

The law of inertia was studied by Galileo and Isaac Newton four centuries ago. It states that objects at rest remain at rest, and objects in motion remain in motion, unless a force is applied. Note that this is a description of nature and not a fundamental explanation, which is still lacking in the science realm.

The root meaning of the word *inertia* is "lazy" or "sluggish." All objects, including coins, have inertia. Thus they tend to resist sudden motion. If time permits, this activity can be made more dramatic. It involves a small tablecloth (without a hem), dishes, a glass, and silverware. Use a small table covering, about four feet by four feet, and dishes that are somewhat heavy (and inexpensive). For added effect, fill the glass with water. When preparations are complete, take hold of an edge of the table covering with both hands. Add to the suspense by acting unsure of yourself. Pull it slowly to show that everything moves. Then quickly jerk the tablecloth off the table in a downward direction. As with the coin, the place setting should be left undisturbed. Practice this activity ahead of time, as always.

# Sink or Swim

**Theme:** God knows our hearts.

**Bible Verse:** All the nations will be gathered before Him, and He will separate them one from another, as a shepherd divides his sheep from the goats. (Matthew 25:32)

**Materials Needed:**
- Aquarium or deep, clear bowl
- Water
- Assorted unopened soda cans, diet and regular

## Bible Lesson

Matthew writes of a future time when those who know the Lord will be selected from all the people of the earth. Scripture is very clear that this day of judgment will come. For the believer this is a great encouragement: someday justice will prevail on the earth. For the unbeliever this promise should be a great motivation to turn to God.

It is impossible for us to judge the motives and hearts of others. We see only the outside of a person, but God looks within the heart and mind. He certainly knows us better than we know ourselves. His judgment is 100 percent accurate and fair.

## Science Activity

This activity compares the densities of several kinds of canned soda. The unopened cans are dropped one at a time into the water-filled aquarium. A little showmanship is in order. You could have the audience guess which cans will float or sink as you drop them in.

A pattern will quickly be noticed: cans of diet soda usually float while the others sink. There may be some rare exceptions if a particular can is not completely filled with liquid. The activity is fun and would probably make a good soft drink commercial! It shows how readily the cans can be separated into categories by using the property of density or weight, which is not obvious from the outside appearance.

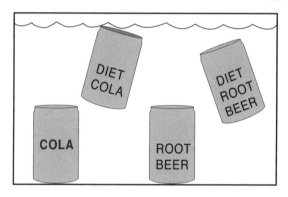

Cans of diet soda float in water while the sugared variety sinks to the bottom.

## Science Explanation

Most diet sodas are sweetened with NutraSweet, also known as aspartame. This artificial sweetener is lighter in weight than the sugar in ordinary soda. Soda cans are not completely filled with liquid; a small amount of carbon dioxide gas is noticeable by the fizzing sound when a soda can is opened. In diet soda, the gas and the aspartame result in a product that is less dense than the aquarium water; therefore the can floats. Meanwhile, the sugared soda is heavier and sinks to the bottom of the aquarium. In a random sample of several cans of soda, I found that the sugared variety averaged 5 percent heavier than the diet.

# Tornado in a Bottle

**Theme:** We should turn our lives over to the one who is in charge of his creation.

**Bible Verse:** Then He arose and rebuked the wind, and said to the sea, "Peace, be still!" And the wind ceased and there was a great calm. (Mark 4:39)

**Materials Needed:**
- Two 2-liter clear plastic soda bottles
- Short section of tubing or hose, or duct tape
- Water
- Bits of paper or plastic

## Bible Lesson

The Sea of Galilee is well known for its sudden storms. Strong winds often descend from the surrounding hills and violently stir up the waves. One day Jesus and the disciples were crossing the sea. While Jesus slept, a storm arose that threatened to sink the boat and drown them all. When Jesus was awakened, he quickly calmed the wind and waves by his word alone. The storm disappeared even more quickly than it arrived. The disciples were amazed at the Lord's obvious power over nature. This is the same Lord whom we are invited to love and serve today. "Salvation is found in no one else, for there is no other name under heaven given to mankind by which we must be saved" (Acts 4:12 NIV).

## Science Activity

Fill one clear, 2-liter soda bottle about three-quarters full with water. Connect a similar bottle to it so that they are somewhat in the shape of an hourglass. A threaded coupling can sometimes be purchased in gift shops for this purpose; a 2-inch section of large tubing or garden

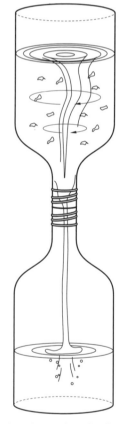

A "mini tornado" can be formed inside two plastic bottles as water swirls between them.

hose will also work. The commercial connector usually has a small, ⅜-inch constriction that extends the time it takes for the water to move from one bottle to the other. This can also be accomplished by leaving one bottle cap on and drilling a hole in the cap. For one-time use, the two bottles can be connected using duct tape or masking tape to firmly wrap their openings together.

When the bottles are inverted and the upper one is moved rapidly in a small circle, a tornado-like swirling begins as the water pours through the neck to the lower bottle. The emptying process takes about thirty seconds and is fascinating to watch. Some small paper or plastic confetti pieces added to the water will enhance the visual effect.

Once the whirlpool begins, it becomes quite vigorous and uncontrolled. The swirling action will continue until the water completely drains to the lower bottle. This small "storm" cannot be stopped, even though it is confined to a plastic bottle. Contrast this with the dangerous storm on the Sea of Galilee, which Christ stopped instantly.

## Science Explanation

The water passing between the bottles undergoes turbulent motion. In science this term describes the complicated swirling motion of liquids or gases. It occurs in ocean currents, in clouds, and within various pipelines. Turbulence is not well understood scientifically. The shape and motion of the whirlpool within the bottles cannot be predicted. That is, equations are not available to exactly describe the motion. Turbulence remains one of the great unsolved problems of physics.

It sometimes appears that science has all the answers, and scientific findings are often presented with dogmatism and aloofness. In truth, every scientific discovery gives rise to multiple new and unanswered questions. And some areas, such as turbulence, may simply remain beyond understanding. However, the Creator has complete knowledge and control of nature, whether the mighty ocean currents or a "tornado" within a bottle.

# Creating a Picture

**Theme:** People, made in the image of their Creator, are a special part of creation.

**Bible Verse:** But from the beginning of the creation, God "made them male and female." (Mark 10:6)

**Materials Needed:**
- Poster board (any color)
- Ruler
- Scissors
- Pencils

## Bible Lesson

There is a popular assumption today in science that we somehow evolved from animals. We are said to be an advanced form of animal, really no different from all other forms of life on the earth. Our key verse makes clear the error of this thinking. From the beginning, mankind has been a unique part of creation. Not only are we separate from the animal world, but we have been given charge over the animals (Genesis 1:26).

Many differences exist between people and animals. Humans have complex languages, a sense of history, and accumulated knowledge through our generations. Another area of our uniqueness is artistic creativity. We have been blessed with minds that can produce an unending variety of beautiful music and works of art. Animals do not have this ability. A robin has a particular song that is beautiful but largely unchanging. Its nest is intricate but is the same design season after season. The robin is programmed to instinctively do robin-like activities. It simply is not capable of experimenting with new songs or new types of nests. So it has ever been for robins and for other kinds of animals since creation. Beautiful spider webs and flowers show *God's* handiwork, not that of the animals and plants themselves. Human creativity truly sets us apart, further showing our special creation in God's image. After all, he is the great Artist and Creator, and he stamped his image upon us.

## Science Activity

Participants will experiment with a tangram puzzle. They can either cut out their own puzzle or be provided with the pieces. The figure shows how to cut a square into seven pieces. Begin with a square of cardboard with 6-inch sides. Draw two diagonal lines that connect the opposite corners of the square. Mark off one diagonal into four equal lengths. Then draw the other lines as shown before cutting out the pieces. If puzzle pieces are prepared ahead of time, have participants solve the puzzle of building a perfect square using the seven pieces.

Now it is time to be creative. Challenge participants to create biblical pictures using all seven pieces, such as a cross, church, star, candle, camel, or whale. Various letters and designs can also be formed. There are thousands of possible pictures. The participants can try to guess each other's creative designs. Remind them that this simple activity illustrates our unique difference from the animal world. We are a special creation. All forms of life have a common Creator, not a common evolutionary ancestor.

## Science Explanation

The tangram is a Chinese game that stimulates thinking. During the 1800s, this puzzle was very popular throughout the United States and

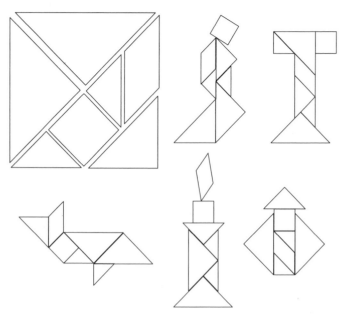

The tangram is a puzzle that takes many forms. Shown are the puzzle pieces and several pictures.

the world. An 1844 British children's magazine complained about young people who wasted hours on the Chinese puzzle to little purpose! Elaborate ivory carvings of the puzzle are now valuable antiques.

Puzzle pieces include a square, rhomboid, and five triangles. The goal is to use all seven pieces to make a design or figure. Entire books have been written to show the possible patterns. I have not yet been able to construct a symmetric cross. Can you? The figure shows some typical results.

# Not Enough Pull

**Theme:** God is able to save us.

**Bible Verse:** But Jesus looked at them and said, "With men it is impossible, but not with God; for with God all things are possible." (Mark 10:27)

**Materials Needed:**
- Two plungers with long handles

## Bible Lesson

Jesus had just told his disciples that it was difficult for a rich man to enter the kingdom of God. In fact, it would be easier for a camel to pass through the eye of a needle. The disciples were astonished at this apparent impossibility. Mark 10:27 records Jesus's reply to the disciples' confusion.

In truth it is impossible for anyone to enter the kingdom of God on his or her own merit. No matter how good we are, we all fall far short of God's perfection. No matter how much money we have or give away, we cannot buy a ticket into heaven. Now the good news: with God all things are possible, including our salvation. What we cannot do, God freely does for us by his love and grace.

## Science Activity

This activity involves a tug-of-war. Push two plungers firmly together. The challenge is to pull them apart again. Perhaps two people can grasp each plunger. Have them sit on the floor so no unexpected falls occur. Participants will quickly find that it is nearly impossible to separate the plungers by pulling outward. It seems to be an impossible task, like the kind of predicament that perplexed the Lord's disciples.

To separate the plungers, simply turn them so the handles are at right angles to each other. Air should then seep between the rubber seals and allow them to easily fall apart. What formerly seemed impossible is actually quite simple. Make clear to the audience that this is a very limited analogy to Mark 10:27. When we know the secret we can separate the plungers. However, gaining salvation by ourselves truly is impossible; there is no simple shortcut. Our eternal life is possible only through Christ's sacrifice for us.

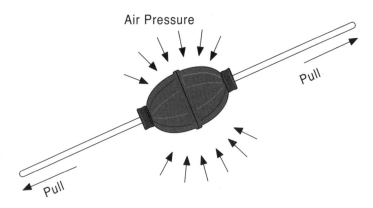

Two joined plungers make a good tug-of-war activity.

## Science Explanation

A famous activity was performed in 1654 in Magdeburg, Germany. Scientist Otto von Guericke brought sixteen horses and two large copper bowls before the emperor. The metal bowls, each about two feet in diameter, were placed snugly together with a leather fitting. The inside air was then removed with a hand pump. Eight horses were harnessed to each copper hemisphere in an effort to pull them apart;

they barely succeeded. This dramatic activity showed the surprising effect of air pressure. With no air or pressure inside the copper hemispheres, the weight of the outside air pushed the spheres together with many tons of force.

When two plungers are pushed together, the inside air is expelled. A plunger that is five inches in diameter has an outside surface area of about forty square inches. Each square inch of the outside surface experiences a force from the air pressure of about fifteen pounds. Thus the plungers are held together by an invisible force of several hundred pounds. It is no wonder that the tug-of-war does not easily succeed. When the plungers are turned at right angles, the inside vacuum is broken, outside air is admitted, and the pressure difference then disappears.

# An Empty Heart

**Theme:** Our lives are controlled either by good or by evil forces; the choice is ours.

**Bible Verse:** When an unclean spirit goes out of a man, he goes through dry places, seeking rest; and finding none, he says, "I will return to my house from which I came." (Luke 11:24)

**Materials Needed:**
- Glass jar with a semi-narrow neck, 1½ to 2 inches across and at least quart-size
- Hard-boiled, shelled egg
- Cotton ball (do not use cotton-like polyester balls)
- Extended lighter or camp lighter

(Perhaps better done on a noncarpeted area)

## Bible Lesson

In Luke 11:24–26 (and also Matthew 12:43–45) Jesus describes a man who has been freed from an evil spirit. Although his life is swept clean, this man does not replace the former evil with the new presence of the Holy Spirit. Instead his heart is left empty and vulnerable to reinvasion. The evil spirit then returns with seven others, and soon the man is worse off than he was before. When God's Spirit does not reside within a person, evil will surely fill the vacuum. It does no good to attempt to clean up one's life if the evil is not replaced with good. In fact, as Scripture shows, the situation may grow worse. We must fill our hearts and minds with the things of the Lord so that he may have control.

## Science Activity

This activity is dramatic and fun. Obtain an empty glass jar (fruit juice, for example) with an opening somewhat smaller than a shelled, hard-boiled egg. Most glass containers have been replaced by plastic, so you may need to check store shelves. The jar represents a person's heart, and the egg represents an evil spirit. Air will be removed from the jar to "sweep it clean." As a result, the egg will then be sucked into the empty jar.

First, show the group that the egg is too large to be pushed inside the jar. Pull and twist the cotton ball into a length that will easily fall into the jar. Cotton is recommended instead of paper since the burning cotton results in negligible smoke or odor. Now ignite the cotton with the lighter and drop it into the jar, pushing the cotton with the extended lighter if needed. Next, quickly and carefully place the egg on top of the jar, smaller end pointed downward. At first hot air will be expelled from the jar and the egg will vibrate up and down. You may have to steady the egg at this time so it doesn't jump completely off the jar. Within seconds, however, the air will be consumed inside the jar and the flame will go out. The remaining air will cool and contract, resulting in a smaller inside air pressure. At this point, the greater outside air pressure will quickly push the egg down inside the jar with a loud burping sound. You might comment on how evil similarly returns to enter an empty heart.

The egg can also be removed from the jar. First, hold the jar upside down and shake it until the egg covers the opening. You may have to withdraw the burned cotton or push it out of the way. Still holding the bottle upside down, give a sharp upward blow of air into it. The air should move past the egg, increasing the inside air pressure and sending the egg flying back out of the jar. Move quickly out of the way after blowing in the jar, or you may get hit by the egg. Explain that evil (the egg) must be replaced by God's presence (the breath of air).

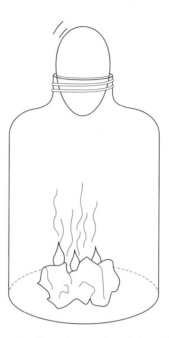

A peeled hard-boiled egg placed over the opening of a jar with burning cotton inside will be pushed into the jar.

## Science Explanation

The egg-in-the-bottle activity is often misunderstood. It is commonly thought that the flame uses up all the air inside the jar, leading to a vacuum. However, this is not the case. In the burning process, oxygen combines with carbon to form carbon dioxide gas, $CO_2$, which is not a vacuum.

Actually, heat is responsible for the vacuum effect. When the inside air is heated, its volume increases two or more times. This increase readily escapes from the jar around the sides of the egg. The egg serves as a flexible, one-way valve that lets air out of the jar but not back in. Then, when the flame is extinguished, the inside air quickly cools and contracts. Outside air then pushes the egg into the resulting partial vacuum within the jar. I demonstrate this egg activity in a YouTube video describing weather details. You will find the experiment at the 17-minute mark. Search for "Weather Insights with Dr. Donald DeYoung" on YouTube.com.

# Walking on Eggshells

**Theme:** God tenderly cares for us.

**Bible Verse:** Are not five sparrows sold for two copper coins? And not one of them is forgotten before God. (Luke 12:6)

**Materials Needed:**
- Several half eggshells
- Masking tape
- Scissors
- Several books

## Bible Lesson

Who cares about sparrows? After all, there are billions of these common birds. The answer is that God made them and he also cares for them. Sparrows in Scripture refer to any small bird of the finch family; they are still found throughout Israel. Each sparrow contributes its chirps, beauty, and nonstop activity to our world. Sparrows spend most of their waking hours in search of food. They don't live long; the record for a sparrow in captivity is ten years. God has given all types of birds instinctive knowledge about nest building, egg care, and feeding their young.

God values his children far above sparrows. In fact, he knows the very number of hairs on our heads (Luke 12:7). Just as God provides for the animal world, so he also provides for us. Christians are not on their own in this world; God watches out for us in many ways that we do not realize.

## Science Activity

This activity shows how well the Creator cares for baby birds within their eggshells. Obtain four or five eggshell halves by cracking fresh eggs. Run a strip of masking tape around the broken edges of four egg shells; then trim the edges of the shells smooth and even with scissors. The tape will prevent the shells from cracking; it can be left on or removed after trimming.

Now place the eggshells, all roughly the same height, on a table with the open ends down. These small egg domes provide "legs" for a book that is gently laid upon them. Add additional books to make a stack on the eggshells. Carefully add even more until one of the shells finally collapses. The books should add up to an impressive amount of weight. You might have a strong volunteer pick up the stack of books to demonstrate the effort needed. An eggshell has been shown to support a person who is perfectly balanced on it.

The eggshell provides a strong home for a baby bird. The shell easily withstands the weather and the weight of the sitting mother.

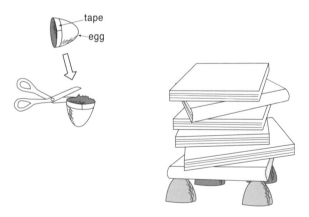

Eggshells will support a heavy load.

The baby emerges by breaking the shell from the inside out. This is a much easier task than breaking an egg from the outside.

## Science Explanation

The dome structure of an eggshell is one of the strongest shapes possible. The thin shell is made of calcium carbonate, $CaCO_3$, which isn't very strong in itself. You might crush an extra eggshell to show participants how fragile they are. However, when the book weight is applied to the top of the dome, the force is transferred along the shell surface to the base. This force tends to compress the eggshell and is strongly resisted. The dome shape is often used as a roof in large stadiums and arenas where supporting columns are not practical.

Here are two other ways to show the strength of an eggshell. If you hold a fresh egg in your palm, it is nearly impossible to crush the egg by squeezing the ends together. Make sure to try this over the kitchen sink, and be careful since the edge of an eggshell can cut. You can also safely toss a fresh egg upward as high as possible above a grassy lawn. The strength of the eggshell and the cushion of grass will almost always prevent the egg from breaking when it lands.

# 54

# Tree Climbing

**Theme:** God designed trees with great strength.

**Bible Verse:** So he [Zacchaeus] ran ahead and climbed up into a sycamore tree to see Him [Jesus], for He was going to pass that way. (Luke 19:4)

**Materials Needed:**
- Sheet of paper (heavy stock if available)
- Tape
- Several paperback books

## Bible Lesson

Zacchaeus was lacking in height but not ambition. When the Lord came his way, Zacchaeus climbed a tree for a better vantage point. Jesus already knew Zacchaeus's name and honored him by visiting his home. As a result, the Zacchaeus family household found salvation.

Trees play a prominent part in Bible history from the Garden of Eden to the cross. Some of the tree identities are uncertain; however, they include the gopher or cypress wood for Noah's ark (Genesis 6:14) and the cedars of Lebanon for King Solomon's temple in Jerusalem (1 Kings 5).

The sycamore fig or fig-mulberry tree in our Bible story is a good climbing tree with spreading branches. It surely was unusual for Zacchaeus, an unpopular businessman, to boost himself up into the tree to see the Lord. One is reminded of the Lord's comment on childlike faith in Luke 18:17. May we likewise be eager to see our Savior.

We can learn much by observing how God made the earth, including the trees. He is, after all, the Great Designer. Let's thank God for creating trees for us to learn from and enjoy.

## Science Activity

Let's explore the design of trees by comparing two paper shapes. Which shape supports more weight, round or square? Fold and then tear in half an 8½" x 11" sheet of paper to make two 8½" x 5½" sheets. Roll one sheet into a cylinder with a bit of overlap and tape the entire seam so that it stands 5½" tall. Put four folds into the other sheet and make a square or rectangle, again with a bit of overlap for taping. The corners should be sharp.

Now let's count how many paperback books the two shapes will support before collapse. Stand the square shape on end and carefully add paperback books to the top. The limit is usually three to six books before the square tower is crushed. Now repeat stacking books for the round shape. The cylinder may be narrower than the square, but it should hold additional books before collapse. It is clear that a round shape supports more weight than flat sides.

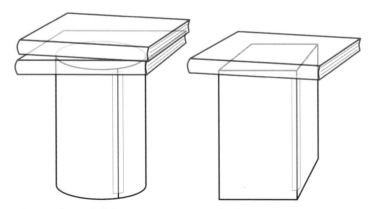

Paper with rounded shape supports more weight than paper with square folds.

Point out that the cylinder shape most closely resembles the trunk and limbs of trees. Participants may suggest other structures in nature with a round shape, including many seashells, flower stems, and bones. The cylinder shape also is found in items we build, such as pencils, canned goods, table legs, water pipes, barrels, some building supports, and barn silos. All are designed for strength.

## Science Explanation

In the case of the square paper shape, the flat sides are the weak links in the structure. When the weight of the books causes a slight twist, one of the sides caves in. In contrast, the round shape has no corners and the weight is shared equally by all parts of the cylinder, giving added strength.

Most trees stand tall and straight for many decades. Their limbs may add up to several tons, yet they remain outstretched during winds, storms, heat, and cold. The giant redwoods in the western United States grow to nearly 400 feet tall, and bristlecone pine trees live for several thousand years. Whether they are young or old, short or tall, trees are a magnificent part of creation.

# A Special Friendship

**Theme:** Christians should give special help and encouragement to each other.

**Bible Verse:** By this all will know that you are My disciples, if you have love for one another. (John 13:35)

**Materials Needed:**
- Strings and weights to make pendulums
- Supports to suspend them

## Bible Lesson

Love is an identifying characteristic of Christians. This is not a mushy, sentimental love, but a deep concern for the welfare of others. It is the opposite of selfishness. We are told to love our neighbors, which means everyone we come in contact with (Matthew 22:39). But John 13:35 describes a special love between believers. This mutual care within the family of God should be clearly visible to the world.

In our day there are many public examples of arguments and lawsuits between Christians and non-Christians alike. People have become skeptical of real love for lack of examples; selfishness is everywhere.

More than ever before, the beautiful testimony of Christian love is needed. It is a bright, guiding light that can attract others to Christ.

## Science Activity

Tie several pendulums to a slack horizontal supporting string, which should be attached to the backs of two chairs placed about four feet apart. Each pendulum has a different length, with just two of them being equal. Lengths between two and three feet will work well. (It is not critical that the pendulums have exactly the same weights suspended on them. One suggestion is to use marbles taped to the strings.)

When one of the equal pendulums is started swinging, the others will vibrate somewhat. However, the matching pendulum will gradually pick up motion, and finally the two will swing together. If the described motion does not occur, try tightening the top supporting string.

If the matched pendulums are not quite equal in length, something else interesting happens: the first pendulum will cease moving altogether, giving all its energy to its partner. Then the process will reverse itself and the original pendulum will slowly regain its motion. The two equal-length pendulums are in resonance, or in tune, with each other.

Christians should support and energize each other as do the two matched pendulums. There is a special bond or connection between

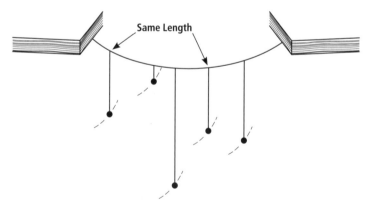

When several pendulums suspended from a slack string are put into motion, the two with equal lengths will swing together.

them. Other people (the remaining pendulums) are not ignored, but there is an obvious link between the true believers. Just as the two equal pendulums energize each other and share their motion, Christians share the love of Christ and also extend it to others.

## Science Explanation

Matched pendulums are said to be in resonance with each other. Since they have the same length and period, they can freely exchange their identical swinging motion. This is not possible for pendulums that are not "in tune" with each other.

There are many related examples of resonance. If a swing is continually pushed in synchronism with its motion, the child will soon be swinging through a high arc (see lesson 73). Also, some cars have a particular speed at which an uncomfortable vibration is felt. There is apparently a resonance coupling between the car's motion on the highway and the car's springs. At speeds below and above this particular value, less vibration is noticed.

# 56

# Walking through Doors

**Theme:** God is not limited by space and location as we are.

**Bible Verse:** Then, the same day at evening, being the first day of the week, when the doors were shut where the disciples were assembled, for fear of the Jews, Jesus came and stood in the midst, and said to them, "Peace be with you." (John 20:19)

**Materials Needed:**
- Sheet of paper 8 ½ " x 11" or smaller
- Scissors

## Bible Lesson

It is clear from the Bible verse that Jesus could pass through closed, locked doors. This was not a mere trick or magic. Jesus's physical body was changed following his resurrection, and he could appear and disappear whenever he wanted. Similar examples are found in John 20:26 and Luke 24. The lesson is clear that Jesus was much more than a man. He was also the Son of God and had supernatural abilities. Jesus is all that he claimed to be; there is no one else equal to him. That is why he deserves all of our attention and praise.

Another lesson is that the Lord is with the believer, wherever that person is. You cannot hide from God, and you are also never beyond his help. This should motivate Christians to live righteously and comfort them in times of trouble. Suppose you were lost in the woods, or locked behind bars, or even exploring deep space. As a Christian, you can be certain that the Lord would also be present; he is never lost or locked out.

## Science Activity

Hold up a sheet of paper and tell your audience that you are going to walk through it. The very idea sounds strange and impossible, but it can be done easily. While you talk, perhaps describing the background of the Bible verse, fold and cut a sheet of paper as shown.

Fold the paper in half lengthwise. Cut slits from the fold, stopping just short of the edges. Now make cuts between the first cuts going from the edges toward the fold and stopping just short of the fold. The narrower the slits are, the better. The cuts are shown in the figure as straight lines. Now open the sheet and cut along the fold, from the first to the last cut (dotted line). Carefully open up the sheet to reveal a large circular ribbon of paper, which you can then easily step through. Practice the cutting process beforehand with scrap paper. If the slits are made close to each other, this trick can even be done with a small index card.

Of course, walking through a sheet of paper is far more artificial than Jesus's ability to pass through closed doors. As with the other activities in this book, the goal is simply to turn our eyes and thoughts to the truth of Scripture. Someday, when believers have glorified bodies, then perhaps they too will be able to walk right through closed doors. The future is indeed exciting for Christians.

## Science Explanation

Suppose an 8½" x 11" sheet of paper is cut as illustrated using ¼-inch strips. When opened up, the ring of paper will be 14 feet around. This is nearly the size of a doorway. A smaller sheet of paper will result in a smaller opening, but one that will still be large enough to slip over your head and shoulders.

You may have heard it said that matter is mostly empty space. Individual atoms indeed have most of their mass concentrated in

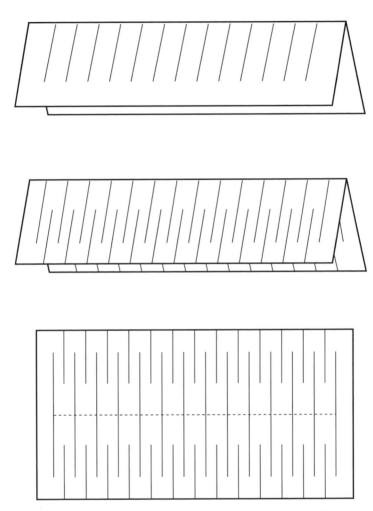

Fold a sheet of paper lengthwise and make overlapping, inward cuts. Open the sheet, cut down the center, and open into a large loop.

the center nucleus. Electrons orbit this nucleus, somewhat similar to planets orbiting the sun. If a scale model were made of an atom using a baseball as the nucleus, then the electrons would be at an outer distance of six miles. That is, electrons are very small and comparatively far from the nucleus. Thus it is true that atoms are mostly empty space.

Some have suggested that the emptiness of matter was somehow rearranged to allow the Lord to walk through closed doors. This may be true, but we must resist the effort to explain the details of miracles. The Lord has supreme power over the physical universe. The ways of the Lord are far beyond our finite understanding (Romans 11:33).

# A Downhill Race

**Theme:** Be faithful to God.

**Bible Verse:** Do you not know that those who run in a race all run, but one receives the prize? Run in such a way that you may obtain it. (1 Corinthians 9:24)

**Materials Needed:**
- Board, such as a table leaf
- Hollow cylinders (paper towel roll, empty soup can)
- Solid cylinders (dowel, thread spool, unopened can of food)
- Solid balls (golf ball, softball, rubber ball, marble)
- Hollow balls (tennis ball, racquetball, ping-pong ball)

## Bible Lesson

The background of our key verse is the great athletic contests that were held during New Testament times. Corinth was where the Isthmian Games took place, a musical festival and athletic competition. The sports included wrestling, discus throwing, and running. This tradition continues today as the Olympic Games.

Most people enjoy competitive sports as either participants or observers. In a race there can be only one first-place winner. And to win, a runner must prepare well, as successful athletes in your audience will readily testify. The prize may only be a ribbon or trophy, but this token is overshadowed by the great honor of finishing first. In Paul's day, the typical prize was a small pine wreath placed on the head of the winner.

Paul points out the great effort and sacrifice necessary to win a competitive prize. Yet far greater is the honor to be gained by being faithful to God. One can tell from the passage that Paul enjoyed sports, but he loved serving the Lord even more. How do we compare with Paul today?

## Science Activity

Everyone likes a race, and you can provide one. The race down a sloping surface will be between four different objects: solid and hollow balls, and solid and hollow cylinders. The group might like to vote on which object will most likely win the downhill race. If the objects are similar in size and weight, the results are predetermined by physical laws of motion.

It may be difficult to have all four objects roll down the board at once. In this case the objects can be released two at a time, with the winner going on to the next round. To start a race fairly, hold the objects at the top, perhaps behind a ruler or yardstick. Then quickly raise the stick without pushing the spheres or cylinders. The race ends at the bottom of the slanted track.

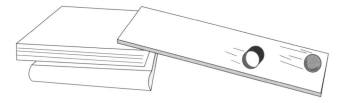

A downhill race between different objects gives predictable results.

## Science Explanation

Various objects falling through the air have similar motion if air resistance is small. So a stone, a book, or a pen all will hit the floor at nearly the same time.

A ramp race involves the rolling of objects, a more complicated process. Here the *shape* of the objects becomes important. Rolling motion is resisted by an object's moment of inertia, given the symbol $I$. This $I$ takes into account the size and distribution of matter within the object itself. Here are some moment of inertia values for several items, where R is the object's radius and M is the object's mass or heaviness:

| Object | $I$ = Moment of Inertia |
| --- | --- |
| Solid sphere | $\frac{2}{5} MR^2$ |
| Solid cylinder or disk | $\frac{1}{2} MR^2$ |
| Hollow sphere | $\frac{2}{3} MR^2$ |
| Hollow cylinder or ring | $MR^2$ |

A solid sphere has the smallest $I$ value, so it will roll the fastest. A hollow cylinder or ring has a large $I$ value and generally lags behind the other shapes. The material that makes up a cylinder or ring is farther away from the rotation axis, and this slows the rolling motion. In contrast, the sphere has more of its mass close to the rotation axis and therefore it turns easily.

# Members of the Family

**Theme:** Each member of the church family is important.

**Bible Verse:** Now you are the body of Christ, and members individually. (1 Corinthians 12:27)

**Materials Needed:**
- Several paper coffee filters
- Scissors
- Washable dark-colored felt-tip pens (black, brown, green, etc.)
- Clear glasses with small amounts of water

## Bible Lesson

Your body is made up of many parts: 206 bones, 100,000 miles of blood vessels, and biological complexity beyond imagination. Every component works together for the benefit of your body. If even one small part fails to perform, however, pain or sickness may quickly result.

The "body of Christ" in 1 Corinthians 12:27 is descriptive of the local church. A congregation is made up of people with various gifts, abilities, and interests. Taken together they contribute to a healthy, functioning church family. No person whom God brings into the local church is more or less important than the others. If one person is missing, the church body is incomplete.

The mark left by a felt-tip pen results from several component colors. Each of these colors is chosen and combined by the manufacturer for the desired result. If any component color is missing, the result will be different. The function of each internal color may not be obvious, but it is very real. Members of the local church family are like the colors within the dyes of the pen. Each is different; each is also essential for the planned result.

## Science Activity

Cut several strips from the coffee filters, each about 1 inch wide and 6 inches long. Give one or more strips to each participant. Now distribute washable felt-tip pens or markers. Have each person draw a dark line across the strip about 1 inch from an end. Strips can be marked with different colors, but black, brown, and green give the most interesting results.

Suspend the paper strip in a glass containing 1 inch of water. The ink line should be about ½ inch above the water level. Make sure the line is not submerged or touching the edge of the glass. Fold the strip over the top edge of the glass or use a pencil to hold it in place. More than one strip can be placed in the same glass as long as they do not touch.

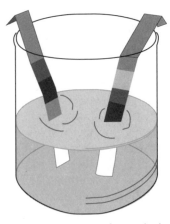

Different inks show a variety of internal color dyes.

Water immediately will begin soaking into the paper and moving upward. In crossing the ink line the water will dissolve color pigments and carry them upward at different rates. Within a few minutes, the components of the ink should be displayed on the upper portions of the paper strip. Compare the strips to see the variety of dyes within the ink. The strips later can be dried and kept as unusual bookmarks.

## Science Explanation

This procedure is called paper chromatography. It is often used to separate pigments that are present in objects such as plant leaves. (In this case place a leaf on the filter paper and roll a coin back and forth over the leaf to leave a green stain.) Capillary action within the absorbent paper draws water upward until it reaches the top of the glass. It is important to use washable pens, or the color separation will not readily occur. Pigments or dyes within the ink are dissolved by the water at different rates. The easily dissolved dyes are carried upward by the water. Less soluble dyes are delayed and remain near the bottom of the paper strip. In this way, a gradual separation of pigments occurs. Some felt-tip colors may have only one pigment. The black, brown, and green, however, are made with a variety of colors. Black pens from different manufacturers may also give different results.

Crime laboratories sometimes use chromatography to separate the components of substances. For example, the particular ink used in a ransom note may be clearly identified in this way, somewhat like a fingerprint.

# Looking in the Mirror

**Theme:** In time we will understand God's plan.

**Bible Verse:** For now we see in a mirror, dimly, but then face to face. Now I know in part, but then I shall know just as I also am known. (1 Corinthians 13:12)

**Materials Needed:**
- Paper
- Pen or pencil
- Square or rectangular mirror (at least 6 inches long)

## Bible Lesson

The city of Corinth was famous in the apostle Paul's time for its production of mirrors. These were polished bronze surfaces, much inferior to modern glass mirrors. The readers of Paul's letter would readily understand the meaning of a poor reflection, compared to one's actual appearance. An unclear mirror image provides an excellent comparison to our present and future understanding of God's plan.

Today we wonder about many things in life:

Why don't we get our own way?

Why is there sickness and pain?

When will the Lord return?

Someday the answers to such questions will be made crystal clear to us. Meanwhile, we can have confidence that God knows what is best for us. God looks down from above and sees all things from beginning to end.

## Science Activity

This activity points out the unusual reflections in a small mirror. Participants are asked to explain what they observe. Various words are printed on paper in capital letters. The words are then reflected in a mirror.

An interesting word pair to begin with is HYMN BOOK. Write this in large letters. Now line up the mirror just above the word, perpendicular to the paper, so you can see both the writing and the reflection. You will find that the word HYMN is upside down while BOOK is unchanged. Why does this happen? Some participants will solve the puzzle quickly; others will not understand the result. Many other words and pictures also give interesting reflections. These examples are especially interesting:

CARBON DIOXIDE

BIKE

RAWHIDE

KITCHEN COOK BOX

LIVE OX

HIDE OR SEEK

You might also have participants write their names and check the reflections. In the end, be sure everyone understands why the reflected words appear as they do. Explain that what was at first a mystery has now become clear. Likewise, God's ways may be poorly understood at present. In time, however, all our questions will be answered.

Some words have unusual reflections in a mirror.

## Science Explanation

Words reflected in the mirror are turned upside down. However, certain letters are shaped so that they are unchanged when inverted. They are symmetric in the vertical direction. These special capital letters are

B, C, D, E, H, I, K, O, X

If lowercase letters are used, the list is reduced to just four:

c, l, o, x

The mirror does not do anything unusual to the words. The letters themselves cause the unusual results.

There are also four numbers that are unchanged when inverted:

1, 3, 8, 0

# The Twinkling of an Eye

**Theme:** At the Lord's command in the end time, all believers on earth will be instantly changed, whether they are dead or alive.

**Bible Verses:** Behold, I tell you a mystery: We shall not all sleep, but we shall all be changed—in a moment, in the twinkling of an eye, at the last trumpet. For the trumpet will sound, and the dead will be raised incorruptible, and we shall be changed. (1 Corinthians 15:51–52)

**Materials Needed:**
- Rulers (one for every two people)

## Bible Lesson

The Lord is very patient with mankind. Nearly two thousand years have passed since Christ physically left the earth and ascended into heaven. However, at his command end-time events could begin on planet Earth. He has power over time and also over death. The above Scripture passage describes events at the conclusion of this age. The bodies of those believers who have died (are "asleep") will be resurrected. Believers who are alive likewise will be instantly changed. Physical death will give way to victory and eternal life through our Lord Jesus Christ (1 Corinthians 15:57).

The event is described as happening in a moment or flash of time. The Greek word used here gives us the modern word *atom*, meaning small and indivisible. The twinkling or briefest movement of an eye describes the supernatural change of the Lord's children. This Scripture promise is a comfort during trials. Someday the Lord will return and make things right. We can rejoice in God's power over nature and look forward to the time when we are changed to be more like him.

For the unbeliever there is no promise of additional time to make a decision for the Lord. There is no assurance of health or life itself from one moment to the next. In a flash, the opportunity for salvation could be lost forever. "Now is the day of salvation" (2 Corinthians 6:2).

## Science Activity

This activity will make us more aware of a brief instant of time. It is a simple technique to measure a person's reaction time, usually a fraction of a second. One person must catch a ruler between his or her separated fingers after it is released by another person. The marks on the ruler will show how many inches the ruler falls before the fingers actually pinch closed and stop the falling ruler. Measure the length that has fallen below the fingers. The following table converts inches of fall into approximate time. The table can be written on a chalkboard or chart.

| Fall of ruler (inches) | Time (seconds) |
|:---:|:---:|
| 2 | 0.10 |
| 4 | 0.14 |
| 6 | 0.18 |
| 8 | 0.20 |
| 10 | 0.23 |
| 12 | 0.25 |

This measurement is fun to make and averages about a 6-inch drop for most people, giving a reaction time of 0.18 seconds. Because of this built-in reaction delay, a person also cannot catch a dollar bill that is held by someone else halfway down between his or her fingers and then dropped. The half-length of a dollar bill is just 3 inches, too short for our typical reaction time. Emphasize the illustration of an instant of time, the mere twinkling of an eye when the ruler falls. The Lord is able to do mighty works on this short time scale.

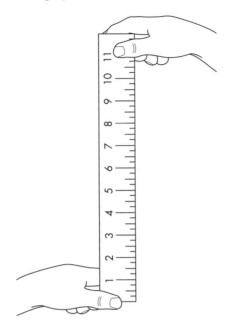

The distance a ruler falls when one person drops it (top hand) and another catches it (lower hand) can be converted to reaction time.

## Science Explanation

At the earth's surface, objects fall because of the downward pull of the earth's gravity. Disregarding air resistance, free fall does not depend on the weight of the object. That is, light and heavy objects will fall with identical motion.

For any free fall distance d, the falling time t can be calculated from the relation

$$t = \sqrt{\frac{2d}{g}}$$

where g is the acceleration due to gravity

g = 32 feet/second$^2$
  = 384 inches/second$^2$

On a larger scale, the formula gives the following times for longer distances:

| Fall distance (feet) | Time (seconds) |
| --- | --- |
| 16 | 1 |
| 32 | 2 |
| 64 | 3 |
| 256 | 4 |

On the moon, where gravity is less, objects fall more slowly, somewhat similar to slow motion. On Jupiter gravity is nearly three times greater than on earth and a dropped ruler would rapidly drop downward.

# Bursting with New Life

**Theme:** Believers must share the gospel.

**Bible Verse:** Therefore, if anyone is in Christ, he is a new creation; old things have passed away; behold, all things have become new. (2 Corinthians 5:17)

**Materials Needed:**
- Handful of hard, dried seeds (pea, bean, corn, or lima bean seeds work well)
- Sand
- Water
- Small clear container that can be sealed, perhaps a glass jar or plastic pill bottle

## Bible Lesson

As growing seeds soak up water, they come alive and can no longer be confined. These seeds illustrate the new believer. When new life is found in Christ, exciting changes will occur. The person can no longer "keep the lid on." Instead, he or she will want to tell others about their new direction. Over time, many positive changes should also be evident in their life.

Once the gift of salvation has been received, who would want to go back to a life that is empty? Likewise, a growing seed cannot be forced back into its original hard shell. Instead, the seed grows and eventually reproduces itself many times over.

## Science Activity

This experiment requires a day or two for completion. Mix seeds and sand in equal amounts. Pour this mixture into a jar, shaking the jar to fill it completely. Now wet the sand thoroughly. Screw the lid on tightly; it need not be airtight. As the seeds absorb water and swell, the expansion will pop the cap from a pill bottle or crack a glass jar. If glass is used, put the container on a cookie sheet to prevent a spill. For a single Bible lesson, the before and after results can be prepared ahead of time to be shown together. If time permits, a container can be loaded up during a lesson and put aside for future inspection. Sometimes seeds swell quickly and may even pop the container during the lesson itself.

Swelling seeds are able to burst almost any container.

## Science Explanation

Seeds can be stored in a dry, dormant form for many years or even centuries. When moisture is present, however, the growth process begins immediately. The seed coat has a small opening, often on an indented side, that admits water. The inner embryo or germ of the seed readily absorbs this water, swelling in the process and cracking its outer shell. In this way the seed begins to produce a root and stem.

The pressure exerted by a growing seed or plant is tremendous. Perhaps you have seen a plant gradually overturn a rock or raise a slab of concrete. Plant growth depends strongly on water movement through small capillary tubes in the plant. It is the changing internal water pressure in the tubes that folds leaves at night and opens blossoms by day. This complex hydraulic action has been operating ever since plants were made on the third day of the creation week.

There is a story, unconfirmed, that the swelling of moist seeds was responsible for the sinking of a supply ship during World War II. A vessel carrying sacks of dried beans was slightly damaged by a torpedo. The ship continued on its way, but the cargo of beans became soaked and started to swell. Eventually, the expansion of the beans split open the hull of the ship, causing it to sink. The vessel survived the torpedo, but not the growth of its cargo of sprouting seeds!

# Lots of Cotton

**Theme:** God blesses us beyond our imagination.

**Bible Verse:** Now to Him who is able to do exceedingly abundantly above all that we ask or think, according to the power that works in us. (Ephesians 3:20)

**Materials Needed:**
- Bag of cotton balls
- Small glasses
- Water

## Bible Lesson

In our minds it is natural to assume that God's power, though great, is limited. Since we often become weary, we therefore think God must likewise tire. Perhaps this is a hidden reason for assuming that the creation week actually must have covered a long period of time. However, God doesn't need our help in this way. He could have completed his universe in a microsecond, drawing upon his infinite reserves of energy. Instead, the creation was accomplished in six literal days, exactly as the book of Genesis states. And God is still able to do more than we can ever ask or think. We should therefore be bold in our prayer requests. Through Christ, this limitless power of God is also within us. Ultimate victory for the Christian is a certainty.

## Science Activity

We will illustrate what appears to be impossible. Show the listeners a small glass nearly filled with water, to within about ¼ inch of the top. On a table there also should be a large pile of fluffy cotton balls. Ask the audience to guess how many cotton balls can be added to the glass before water spills over the top. It appears that only two or three balls should completely fill the glass. However, the actual results are quite surprising. Many cotton balls can be added to the glass, one after another, and no water will spill. Instead, the water is totally absorbed by the cotton, which greatly shrinks in size. Press the cotton balls down firmly together with your fingers to make room for others. I was able to squeeze one hundred cotton balls into a small glass in this way. This large capacity for cotton balls is unexpected. Just as surprising are God's abundant blessings that continue daily.

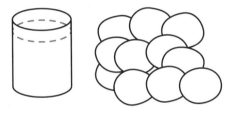

Many cotton balls can be added to a small glass of water that is almost full without spilling any of the liquid.

## Science Explanation

Cotton fibers are largely made of cellulose, the main component of many plants. This complex carbohydrate has the formula $(C_6H_{10}O_5)n$ where $n$ is a large number. The individual cotton fibers are about 1 inch long and only 10–20 microns ($10^{-6}$ meter) in diameter. This is about ten times smaller than the diameter of a human hair. A fluffy cotton ball of fibers is mostly empty space. When compressed, its volume is greatly reduced. The water used in the activity is for visual effect, and it also helps hold the cotton together in a wadded form.

Cotton is the most universal fiber known, used worldwide for making cloth fabric. It is a marvelous gift from the Creator. After the lesson, the cotton balls can be spread out to dry for reuse. However, they will not resume their original fluffiness, even when thoroughly dry.

# A Dependable Universe

**Theme:** God faithfully holds his universe together.

**Bible Verse:** And He is before all things, and in Him all things consist. (Colossians 1:17)

**Materials Needed:**
- Tennis ball (or one similar in size)
- Several feet of string
- Masking tape

## Bible Lesson

Scientists have learned much about the forces of nature. The gravity force keeps us on the ground, and the electric force holds atoms together in all objects. We can write down formulas for these forces, but our understanding remains limited. What really is gravity? What is electric charge? We do not know; these are simply terms for describing what we observe.

Colossians 1:17 implies that Christ established the laws of gravity and electricity, and that he maintains them day by day. Consider the alternative: if the Lord turned his back on the universe for just one moment, instant chaos surely would result. Water, the land, the moon—all would disintegrate. The earth would lose its shape and leave its solar orbit, drifting off into the darkness of space. Christ remains very much in charge of his universe, for our daily benefit. Shouldn't we put all our trust in the One who created and operates the universe?

## Science Activity

Attach the string to the ball with a knot or tape so that it can be swung in a vertical circle, like a large wheel. The ball represents the orbiting earth, with your hand as the sun at the center of the circle. Ask your audience what will happen when you release the string at the top of the ball's arc. Will it go straight up and hit the ceiling, or perhaps drop down and hit you? Count out loud—"one, two, three"—and then release the ball at the top of its loop. Be sure to aim the ball in a clear direction so no one is hit. The motion is similar to that of a stone leaving a sling. The ball will travel on a tangent, in roughly a straight-line direction. This is exactly what the earth would do if gravity suddenly ceased to exist. Our planet would leave the sun behind, and life for us would quickly grow cold, dark, and impossible.

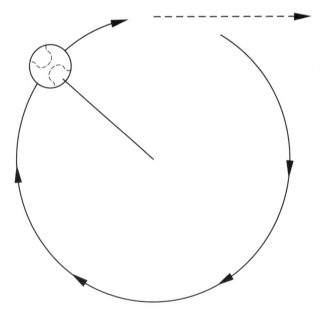

When a ball on a string is swung in a circle and released, it will leave on a nearly straight-line tangent.

## Science Explanation

When the ball is released during its swing, it does not travel on exactly a straight path. Instead, the earth's gravity attraction pulls downward on the ball. As the ball moves horizontally, it follows a parabolic path to the ground. The curvature of this motion is slight enough that it does not interfere with the activity.

Gravity remains a mysterious force in nature. It acts through great distances of empty space. The gravitational attraction between the earth and sun also continually adjusts to the earth's changing location. There is scientific speculation that invisible gravity particles called gravitons, or perhaps gravity waves, continually flow between space objects such as the earth and sun. However, these particles or waves have not yet been detected. We are reminded of Colossians 1:17, which states that God holds all things together, including the moon, earth, sun, and stars.

# Danger—Deep Water

**Theme:** Obey your parents.

**Bible Verse:** Children, obey your parents in all things, for this is well pleasing to the Lord. (Colossians 3:20)

**Materials Needed:**
- Large, clear water glasses
- Water
- Pennies

## Bible Lesson

Cari and her father stood at the edge of the swimming pool looking down into the water. They could clearly see the black lines painted on the bottom. The inviting water looked shallow enough for easy wading, and Cari asked for permission. Dad cautioned her that water is often deeper than it looks, and therefore one must be very careful around pools. They stepped into the water together, and Cari was surprised. The water was indeed deep, and she held on tightly to her dad. The pool, which had looked so friendly a moment ago, was now a place of danger for her.

Cari's father further explained that many people have been fooled by the unexpected depth of water. Lifeguards are trained to watch for safety misjudgments by inexperienced swimmers.

In Cari's eyes the pool was shallow and safe. However, this was an incorrect assumption. She needed her dad's help to avoid the deep water. God has given us parents and other helpful adults to protect us and care for us. Grown-ups have already experienced many of the hazards of life. Their parents once taught them about life's dangers. This valuable pattern of one generation helping the next pleases the Lord. It is *not* a sign of weakness to obey your parents; it is a sign of wisdom.

## Science Activity

This activity shows why Cari was confused by the pool water's depth. Each person or small group is given a glass filled with water. A coin is dropped into the filled glass and then looked down upon from above. A second coin is placed on the table surface close to the glass and also observed from above. The submerged coin will appear to be somewhat elevated and will look closer to your eye than the dry coin. It is an interesting sight: the coins are obviously at the same table level, yet they look quite different.

The water in the glass appears shallower than it actually is, just as is true for any swimming pool. Water depth always acts this way,

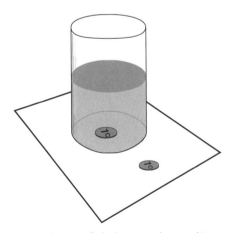

A penny looks magnified when it is submerged in water.

which is actually a mixed blessing. This effect makes diving somewhat safer because water is deeper than it appears; there is more room for underwater clearance. For a child stepping into a pool, however, shallow-looking water that is actually deep can lead to an accident.

## Science Explanation

The *apparent* depth of water is always less than the *actual* depth when you look down from above. This results from the slowdown of the speed of light in water. Light travels only 75 percent as fast in water as in air. Here is a comparison of several water depths:

| Actual depth | Apparent depth |
| --- | --- |
| 6 in. | 4.5 in. |
| 1 ft. | 9 in. |
| 4 ft. | 3 ft. |
| 10 ft. | 7.5 ft. |

In each case the actual depth is multiplied by 0.75 to find the apparent water depth.

Apparent depth results in several other interesting illusions. You may have noticed some of these:

Your legs appear shorter when you stand in water.

Items underwater can be difficult to pick up. They are often not positioned where they appear to be.

A partially submerged oar or paddle often appears to be broken or bent.

A pencil or finger placed in a filled glass and observed from the side appears to be enlarged or magnified.

All these effects result from the slowdown and bending of light in water, also called light refraction.

# Spreading Outward

**Theme:** Run from sin.

**Bible Verse:** But you, O man of God, flee these things and pursue righteousness, godliness, faith, love, patience, gentleness. (1 Timothy 6:11)

**Materials Needed:**
- Bowl
- Water
- Pepper
- Liquid dish soap

## Bible Lesson

There is a time to stay and fight, but there is also a time to flee. Several harmful practices are listed in 1 Timothy 6, including the teaching of false doctrines (v. 3), unhealthy interest in controversies (v. 4), and the love of money (v. 10). Whatever form it may take, the Christian should flee from sin. Like pepper floating on water, we need to stay as far away from temptation as possible.

In contrast, our key verse names the abundant good things we should pursue: righteousness, godliness, faith, love, endurance, and gentleness. These qualities will lead to fulfillment in this life and also the life to come.

## Science Activity

Fill the bowl with water. Give the water a minute to settle and become still. Sprinkle some pepper on the water's surface; it will float like dust particles. Now gently place a drop of liquid dish soap in the center of the surface. (You can also touch a moist finger to a bar of soap, then dip your finger in the bowl.) The soap film should quickly spread out, carrying the pepper particles instantly to the outer edges of the bowl.

The pepper represents a believer, and the soap drop is an evil influence. (Some young children might already think that soap is bad!) The pepper immediately flees the soap as a believer should flee sin.

The depth of water is not important. Other substances such as talcum powder can also be used in place of pepper. However, the dark color of pepper gives it a visual advantage.

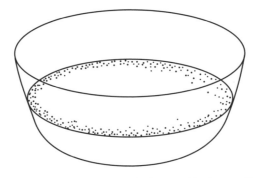

Floating pepper particles are pushed outward by the soap film.

## Science Explanation

When the drop of soap is applied to water, it spreads out like a very thin pancake. The pepper is light enough to be pushed out of the way by the expanding soap film. Soap weakens the surface tension of water (see lesson 66) in the center of the bowl. The unaffected water molecules around the outside edge then pull the pepper specks together.

On a larger surface of water, soap will spread outward in a circle that may be several feet across. The layer becomes as thin as possible, the thickness of a single soap molecule. Benjamin Franklin and other scientists used this technique in the 1700s to estimate the size of individual molecules.

Some activity books recommend using a drop of cooking oil instead of soap. However, I find that soap works best. Within minutes the soap will completely dissolve into the water. This may sink the pepper particles as the soap further breaks down the water's surface tension. Before repeating the experiment, all traces of soap must be washed from the bowl.

# A Bubble of Water

**Theme:** God continually watches over his universe and keeps it operating through his physical laws.

**Bible Verse:** [God is] upholding all things by the word of His power. (Hebrews 1:3)

**Materials Needed:**
- Pennies
- Eyedroppers
- Water
- Paper towels

## Bible Lesson

In science classes we often describe the laws of nature. In truth, however, they are God's laws. They were established at the creation to make our world dependable and fit for life. We also find that the laws of gravity, motion, and energy operate everywhere in space. That is, we live in a *universe* where God's fingerprint of planning is obvious even in faraway places.

If our universe had formed by chance or accident, there would be no certainty that it would continue for another instant. In contrast, our Bible verse gives assurance of God's continual control over nature. It is this promise that makes science research and discovery possible.

## Science Activity

Our activity shows one small but essential part of nature called surface tension. Each participant is given a penny, an eyedropper, a small container of water, and a table or flat surface to work on. The object is to see how many drops of water can be placed on the face of the penny before water overflows the side. (Any kind of straw or squeeze bottle that releases single drops would work instead of eyedroppers.) The surface tension or stickiness of water results in a rounded bead of water on the penny. As water drops are carefully added, the growing bubble or "skin" of water will rise and wobble. The water drops will hold together in an impressive bubble. Eventually, gravity overcomes the water's surface tension and a small spill occurs. Have paper towels nearby for the cleanup. If time permits, have participants count the drops as they are applied to compete with each other for the highest number.

Surface tension allows many drops of water to remain on a penny.

## Science Explanation

Water has one of the highest surface tensions of any common material. In the following comparative list, only mercury has a greater surface tension.

| Liquid | Relative Surface Tension |
|---|---|
| Ethyl alcohol | .29 |
| Ammonia | .31 |
| Soapy water | .33 |
| Sulfuric acid | .73 |
| Blood | .80 |
| Water | 1.0 |
| Mercury | 6.5 |

This high surface tension of water has many practical benefits:

Water climbs up the narrow capillary tubes of plants and trees to water the upper leaves.

Watery fluids cling to our bone joints and also our eyes for constant lubrication.

Surface tension causes raindrop formation.

Soil remains moist as water drops cling to each other and to soil particles.

Water molecules are drawn toward each other because of an attractive electrical force. Slightly positive hydrogen atoms in one water molecule are attracted to negatively charged oxygen atoms in surrounding molecules. This forms a hydrogen bond that is responsible for many of water's special properties.

For further study, add a drop of soap solution to a penny that is covered with water. Soap reduces surface tension, causing the water to quickly spill off the coin. This soap property helps water droplets separate so they can move inside cloth fabric during clothes washing. The water then dissolves dirt and particles within the material fibers and carries them away.

# Piercing the Heart

**Theme:** God's Word shows our need and gives us hope.

**Bible Verse:** For the word of God is living and powerful, and sharper than any two-edged sword, piercing even to the division of soul and spirit, and of joints and marrow, and is a discerner of the thoughts and intents of the heart. (Hebrews 4:12)

**Materials Needed:**
- Two balloons, a light-colored large one and a dark-colored small one
- Large pin or needle

## Bible Lesson

For the Christian, the Bible is a special book. It is God's written Word. We read about the creation of humankind and about successes and failures in the past. Happily we also read about Christ's love for us and his remedy for our sin. As we study the Bible it should cause us to take action. God's Word discloses our inward thoughts and challenges our hearts to faith and upright living. What will we do with this invitation?

## Science Activity

The outer balloon should be large, ten or more inches in diameter, and light colored so it is somewhat transparent. The inner balloon should be smaller and dark colored for visibility. Insert the small balloon into the large one by pushing it inward with the eraser end of a pencil. Then blow up the inner balloon completely and knot the end. This may take some effort. Now inflate the outer balloon, but not fully, and knot it also. The inner balloon should bounce around freely inside.

When it is time for the activity, grasp the large balloon and squeeze it so that the inner balloon is forced up against the top near the nozzle. The underinflated outer balloon will have some flexible "give" around the top, whereas the inner balloon will have a relatively hard surface. If a pin is now slowly pressed deeply against the top of the outer balloon, it will make an indentation without actual puncture. However, the inner balloon should loudly pop. Usually the outer balloon is unharmed; sometimes an unnoticed pinhole is formed. Shake the large balloon to show the fragments from the inner balloon within.

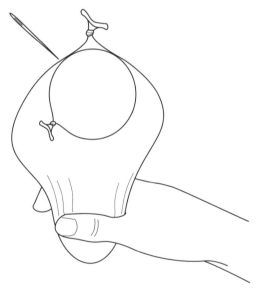

A small, completely inflated balloon inside a large, partially inflated balloon can be popped with a pin from the outside without popping the outer balloon.

The inner balloon represents our inner being. It is hidden by outer appearance (the large balloon). The Lord is not stopped by outside barriers. His Word enters our hearts and probes like the pin that pricks the inner balloon. When we come to know the Lord, the real change takes place on the inside of our lives. The transition from an inflated balloon to small pieces shows how complete and dramatic this change is.

## Science Explanation

A pinprick hole in a balloon becomes a sudden point of weakness. A tear begins and quickly moves across the surface of the balloon with a pop. In engineering terms, this is called progressive failure of the balloon skin.

In this activity, the outer balloon is protected by having a flexible, underinflated skin. It deflects greatly without tearing. Another way to protect the outer balloon is to put a piece of transparent tape on its surface. A needle can then be inserted directly through the tape without destroying the balloon; only a small leak will result.

# Nothing Hidden

**Theme:** God clearly knows whether or not we belong to him.

**Bible Verse:** And there is no creature hidden from His sight, but all things are naked and open to the eyes of Him to whom we must give account. (Hebrews 4:13)

**Materials Needed:**
- Two glass jars or test tubes
- Liquid dish soap
- Hard water and soft water samples

## Bible Lesson

Hebrews 4:12–13 explains that God's Word is powerful. It is a judge of our actions and innermost thoughts. Our standing before God may be evaluated by the standard of Scripture. Verse 13 declares that it is impossible to keep any secrets from God. We may fool others and even ourselves with hidden motives, but everything is on open display before God. He knows who is telling the truth and who is on his side. This is a sober warning but also a comforting thought. God knows what is true and false in this world. He also understands our innermost hurts and fears. In fact, he knows us better than we know ourselves.

## Science Activity

This lesson makes visible something that is usually unseen. The example given here is both easy and familiar. Two kinds of water are needed: hard and soft. In many places groundwater is naturally hard because of dissolved calcium, magnesium, or iron. Because these atoms are in solution, they are invisible to the eye. Bottled mineral water will also suffice. Softened water is available in many homes. Rain or distilled water can also be used for soft water. The two types of water, hard and soft, look identical. We cannot easily tell them apart, although there is a large internal difference. Likewise, people may be similar in outward appearance. We cannot see within the heart to determine what a person really stands for, but God can.

Put the two water types into separate jars or test tubes, about half full. (So that a large group can see the activity, use 2-liter, clear plastic soda bottles.) Add a few drops of liquid dish soap to each container. Now, with the tops sealed, simultaneously shake the two containers

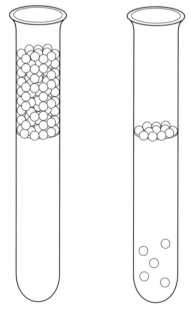

A container with soap and soft water (left) looks different than one with soap and hard water (right).

equally for about thirty seconds. The difference between the two water types should now be obvious:

The impurities in the hard water prevent the soap from performing properly. Instead, a messy white precipitate forms, sometimes known as bathtub ring. The pinch of soap dramatically reveals the difference in the water types. Our inner, hidden thoughts are just as open and apparent before God's eyes.

## Science Explanation

If samples of hard and soft water are left out in the open to evaporate for a couple days, the difference becomes obvious. White scale material forms around the sides of the evaporating hard water. This white residue consists of calcium, magnesium, or iron. It is actually dissolved rock powder that precipitates with the loss of water.

The use of hard water may lead to a number of difficulties. The soap-hardness precipitate may leave a gummy residue behind during hair washing. In cooking, hard water will make food taste slightly "tough." Over time, hard water buildup may completely plug hot-water pipes. This extended lesson application shows the difficulties that develop and grow when problems are not dealt with.

If hard water is not available, you can make your own by adding a pinch of epsom salts (magnesium chloride) to water. One other tip is that the water comparison activity works with liquid dish soap but not with powdered detergent. Powdered detergents are formulated to minimize suds in dishwashers and clothes washers.

# What Is Faith?

**Theme:** Deep theological discussion of faith is interesting, but the simple faith of a child is completely effective for knowing God.

**Bible Verse:** Now faith is the substance of things hoped for, the evidence of things not seen. (Hebrews 11:1)

**Materials Needed:**
- Banana
- Needle and thread

## Bible Lesson

Many unbelievers are unfamiliar with the concept of faith. In this skeptical age, people claim not to trust in anything or in anyone beyond themselves. In contrast, the very word *faith* means belief or trust, especially in God. Hebrews 11, the great faith chapter, illustrates the concept.

What is faith? First, it is being sure. Faith results in complete confidence in the object of one's trust (v. 1). Second, faith is the key to understanding the creation of the universe (v. 3). Miracles such as creation cannot be comprehended, but they can be believed and appreciated. Third, faith is not an easy shortcut for unthinking people.

Hebrews 11 is a roll call of honor for early believers who bravely displayed outstanding faith in difficult circumstances.

Faith in Christ is both the condition of salvation and one of its results. That is, through Christian growth and Bible study, faith will become ever deeper and richer. Faith is a great blessing of the Christian life. Let us give thanks for this precious gift.

## Science Activity

No study could ever plumb the depths of Christian faith. This particular activity challenges the listeners in just one area: believing something they cannot see and that is, in fact, doubtful to them. Hold up a banana and ask if anyone could possibly believe that it is completely sliced, even though it has not been peeled. Real faith involves the action of stepping out and making a commitment; are there any volunteers? Of course, the idea sounds impossible. Who has ever seen an unpeeled banana already sliced? However, faith sometimes involves seemingly impossible events such as creation, miracles, and the resurrection. Continue an open discussion concerning the banana and faith:

Perhaps genetic presliced bananas have been developed.

Has anyone ever peeled a banana and found it already sliced?

If people want to inspect the banana, they may.

Tell the group it is sliced, and see if anyone will believe you.

Finally, peel the banana and show that it is indeed presliced. Sometimes, faith in unseen things is entirely appropriate.

It is only fair to tell the group how you did the "trick." There are two ways to preslice a banana. The quick method is to insert a long, thin needle straight into the banana along a ridge. Push the needle from side to side, slicing through the soft inside. By feeling the outside of the banana, you can tell when the needle is cutting completely through the inside without tearing the outer peeling. When the needle is finally pulled out, its puncture mark should not be noticeable. Repeat this process several more times along the ridge until the inner banana is completely sliced along its length. Keep the needle clean so you can eventually eat some slices before the group. Practice this procedure ahead of time and inspect the results by peeling the bananas.

The second slicing method is more ingenious but also takes a bit longer. This time a needle with strong thread is pushed through the banana just under the peel, along a flat surface segment. Then the needle is reinserted into the next segment the same way, and on around the outside. The thread is finally drawn back out the original puncture hole. Finally, as the thread is pulled out, it will slice through the banana. As before, this process is repeated several times along the banana's length. The result once again is a presliced, unpeeled banana.

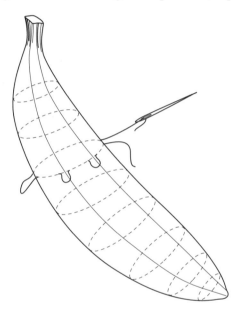

A needle and thread can slice an unpeeled banana.

## Science Explanation

Genetic engineers are striving to produce new food items: square tomatoes for easier packaging and strawberries as large as apples. However, a presliced banana is not yet available! This activity can also be performed with an apple, slicing it from the inside out using a needle or straight pin.

# 70

# Losing Excess Weight

**Theme:** We must be careful not to get involved with things that hinder our service to God.

**Bible Verse:** Therefore we also, since we are surrounded by so great a cloud of witnesses, let us lay aside every weight, and the sin which so easily ensnares us, and let us run with endurance the race that is set before us. (Hebrews 12:1)

**Materials Needed:**
- Swivel chair
- Two heavy objects (books, weights, rocks, etc.)

## Bible Lesson

The great cloud of witnesses in Hebrews 12:1 includes the group of heroes listed in chapter 11. These men and women gave the Lord first place in their lives. They were by no means perfect, but their faith helped them succeed in life. God likewise has a plan and purpose for each of us. We choose to either fulfill this plan or frustrate it. Hebrews 12:1 reminds us to keep our eyes on the goal of serving God with whatever talents and resources he has given to us.

A once popular army ad challenged the viewer to "Be all that you can be." In real life that goal is only accomplished by heeding Hebrews 12:1 and giving God priority. This certainly does not mean that we must give up all our hobbies or recreation time. It does mean that we should consider how we spend our time and how involved we are with temporary, material things.

## Science Activity

A swivel chair is needed, one that turns easily. Have a volunteer slowly spin around while holding two weights with arms extended. As the

A person spins around on a swivel chair while holding weights with the arms extended. When the weights are drawn inward the turning motion speeds up.

person is freely turning he or she now pulls the weights inward, close to the body. There will be a noticeable increased speed of the spinning motion. The turning motion can be slowed again by extending the weights outward. It gives an interesting turning sensation, and others might like to try it also.

The turning effect involves the conservation of angular momentum. When rotating objects are drawn inward toward the center of motion, speed always increases as a result. We have all seen this done by figure skaters. The application is that just as extended weights slow us down, so the details of life can entangle us and hinder our service to God.

## Science Explanation

Angular momentum (L) for a rotating object can be calculated from the relation $L = mwr$. The moving object's mass is m, angular speed w is in radians per second, and radial distance from the rotation axis is r. In the absence of any external torque on a rotating object, the object's angular momentum remains constant.

In the activity, the radial distance is decreased by pulling the weights inward. Then, since angular momentum and mass do not change, the angular speed increases and the person will turn faster.

There are several basic conservation laws in nature that describe constant quantities. These include conservation of angular momentum, linear momentum, energy, and electric charge. Through experimentation, each of these quantities has been found to exactly obey laws of constancy. The existence of these important rules is a powerful testimony to the planning and sustaining work of the Creator.

# Silly Putty

**Theme:** An unstable person is of two minds—unsure whether or not to trust God.

**Bible Verse:** He who doubts is like a wave of the sea driven and tossed by the wind . . . he is a double-minded man, unstable in all his ways. (James 1:6, 8)

**Materials Needed:**
- Cornstarch
- Water
- Popsicle or stir sticks
- Tablespoon measure
- Coffee mugs
- Small plastic bags

## Bible Lesson

James 1:5 invites the believer to ask God for wisdom and understanding about daily decisions. There is one requirement for this help, however. The request must be made with no wavering or doubt (v. 6). A doubter is not sure whether God hears him or if God even understands his plight. Such a man is double-minded; he attempts to divide his trust between God and himself.

This unfortunate person can be humorously compared to Silly Putty. The strange material does not keep its shape but always tends to flow downward. The putty has no strength; it can easily be twisted, bounced, or flattened. Silly Putty is unstable and cannot be trusted to maintain its shape. Likewise, the unstable person cannot be trusted as an example to follow because he lacks the balance of God's wisdom.

## Science Activity

The participants will make their own "Silly Putty," an amusing rubbery substance. Have each participant follow this recipe:

> Place about ½ cup of cornstarch in each mug. Put newspaper under the mug to catch any spills. Now slowly add water, stirring with the popsicle stick. Add water until a gooey, fluid-like consistency results. If too much water is added, additional cornstarch will thicken the material. Fingers can also be used in mixing. You have now made your own form of Silly Putty, which can be pulled from the cup.

This interesting material can be stretched and shaped, but it will slowly spread out and flatten when left on its own, somewhat like thick syrup. Place a small heavy object on the putty and watch it begin to sink out of sight. When quickly pulled apart, the putty will break like plastic. If pressed against a newspaper the putty also may pick up some of the print.

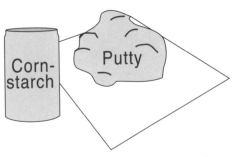

Homemade Silly Putty displays unusual properties.

## Science Explanation

The putty is a suspension of cornstarch in water. This material has dual properties of both a solid and a liquid. It flows like a liquid but can also be broken and pulled apart. It appears wet but becomes powdery if rubbed between your fingers. This putty withstands the sudden shock of being hit, but it cannot support the weight of objects laid upon it. Other familiar non-Newtonian fluids, as they are called, are paint, ketchup, and commercial Silly Putty. Although this putty is nontoxic, participants should wash their hands afterward. If placed in a pocket or on furniture, the putty will slowly enter the fabric. In such cases it can be dissolved away with warm water. The putty can be stored in a closed plastic bag. After prolonged storage the putty may develop mold—discard it if this occurs.

Silly Putty originated in 1943, through efforts to make synthetic rubber during World War II. James Wright, a Dow Corning engineer, first made Silly Putty. He put this new material away on the shelf, thinking it a poor substitute for rubber. Later, someone realized that the putty made a cute toy. Introduced on the *Howdy Doody* television program in 1957, Silly Putty quickly became a national fad. More recently, the putty has been useful as a grip strengthener and also as an art medium.

# Turning a Ship

**Theme:** The power of the tongue must be used wisely.

**Bible Verse:** Look also at ships: although they are so large and are driven by fierce winds, they are turned by a very small rudder wherever the pilot desires. Even so the tongue is a little member and boasts great things. See how great a forest a little fire kindles! (James 3:4–5)

## Materials Needed:
- Water glass
- Two-liter clear plastic soda bottle or juice container
- Water
- Plastic drinking straw
- Several paper clips

## Bible Lesson

The Johnsons were on vacation and were aboard a large car ferry headed to an offshore island. This was ten-year-old Scott's first ride on a large boat, and he enjoyed every detail. However, all the surrounding water was a bit frightening. The feeling was not helped when he saw another ferry in the distance coming straight toward them. *I'm sure these ferries have made the trip hundreds of times,* thought Scott. *But what if they should collide today when we are on board?*

Scott's father saw him staring at the other ferry and realized Scott's concern. Dad asked Scott if he knew how a captain steered his boat. "Is it like a car's steering wheel?" guessed Scott. Dad then explained that steering a boat in water involves a rudder. It is like holding a paddle in the water to turn a canoe. A ship's rudder likewise will turn the boat to the left or right.

By now the other ferry was passing by at a safe distance. They could see the top portion of its rear rudder, which guided the boat's path. The rudder's small size was surprising on such a large ferry. Dad reminded Scott of James 3:4–5, where a ship rudder is compared with the tongue. Both are powerful steering agents. Words can steer people either in right or wrong directions. "Just as the two ferries passed safely," said his father, "let's be sure that our words are also safely used toward others."

## Science Activity

This activity is a team project to build a *Cartesian diver*. The diver is a small object that can be made to either float or sink in the water-filled plastic jar. A popular science project, Cartesian divers are typically made using an eye dropper or test tube. The diver we will make is a plastic straw bent in half. After bending the straw, connect the two end openings together with a paper clip.

The goal is to weight the bent straw with additional paper clips until the straw stays just afloat at the surface of a water-filled glass with the paper clips toward the bottom. For extra weight you can also pour a bit of water into the straw itself.

Next, fill the large plastic container to the brim with water. Drop in the straw "diver" and tighten the cap on the bottle. The bent straw should float at the top. If you now firmly squeeze the sides of the plastic jar, the diver should sink to the bottom. When you release the sides of the jar, the diver should again rise to the top. This motion can be repeated by others. It may be useful to have a second Cartesian diver made ahead of time since some divers are more sensitive than others in responding to pressure on the sides of the jar.

The motion of the straw is an analogy with James 3:4–5, only with an underwater diver instead of a surface ship. The diver is easily steered upward or downward in the water by squeezing the jar. Our control of the diver is a reminder of how we must control our words since they can have a great impact on others.

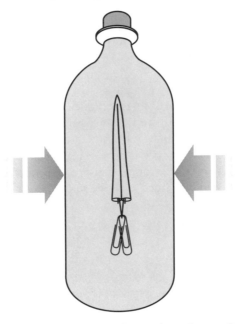

The position of the Cartesian diver can be easily controlled.

## Science Explanation

The Cartesian diver was invented by the French scholar René Descartes (1596–1650). Science activity books describe many ways to build a diver. I have found the bent straw to be the simplest method. The diver rises and falls due to pressure changes. Pushing inward on the sides of the plastic bottle slightly increases the pressure throughout the water. Whatever object is used to make the diver, it must be open at its bottom. Increased pressure pushes water upward inside the diver, compressing the air bubble inside. In this way the diver becomes heavier than water and sinks. If carefully balanced, a very slight pressure change is sufficient to move the diver up or down.

# Moving a Mountain

**Theme:** A faithful life, in prayer and in practice, brings results.

**Bible Verse:** Confess your trespasses to one another, and pray for one another, that you may be healed. The effective, fervent prayer of a righteous man avails much. (James 5:16)

**Materials Needed:**
- Heavy weight
- Strong cord
- Small hammer

## Bible Lesson

James 5:16 reminds us that there is great power in prayer. Fervent prayer is steady, unhurried, and sincere. It is offered with full confidence of results. Using a prayer list illustrates fervent prayer. Items are prayed for on a daily basis, answered prayers are marked off as victories, and new items are added as they arise. If we only realized the true power of prayer, even (or especially) that of a child, it would surely change our lives.

## Science Activity

We will show how a small but steady effort can result in a major change. A heavy pendulum is needed—a weight such as a bucket of water or a piece of metal suspended from the ceiling. A ceiling hook for hanging plants may provide support. The cord should be carefully measured so that the total length from the top support to the center of the weight is 39 inches. Any pendulum with this length will swing with a time period of exactly two seconds. The actual amount of the weight does not matter. If the weight is tapped once every two seconds by hand or a small hammer, it will slowly accumulate motion and soon be swinging widely. The process is similar to steadily pushing or pumping a swing to a high level.

With a little practice, you can easily tap the pendulum with the two-second rhythm. The many small taps will be gradually transferred into a much larger motion. Perhaps you will not move a mountain, but you will move something heavy. In a similar way, a consistent Christian life of prayer can lead to major results for God's glory. Success does not only go to the swift and the strong but also to the faithful. Never underestimate the influence of a consistent Christian life.

This pendulum activity was once performed with a heavy suspended steel beam that was struck regularly by a small cork on a string. After ten minutes a slight vibration could be seen. After half an hour the entire beam swung like a mighty pendulum.

Your particular situation may require a different length of pendulum. The following table shows other lengths and corresponding time periods for one complete swing. One time period is a complete back-and-forth swing.

| Length (inches) | Time (seconds) |
|---|---|
| 10 | 1 |
| 39 | 2 |
| 61 (5' 1") | 2.5 |
| 88 (7' 4") | 3 |
| 156 (13' 0") | 4 |
| 243 (20' 3") | 5 |

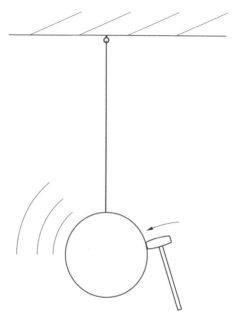

Tapping a large suspended object at regular intervals with a small object results in the large object swinging widely.

## Science Explanation

Suppose a heavy pendulum is tapped by a small force of just one ounce, once each second. After one minute the combined force will be almost four pounds. After five minutes the force will total almost nineteen pounds. In this way a small, steady push slowly increases in influence.

The list of pendulum lengths $\ell$ and swinging periods T was calculated from the pendulum equation

$$T = 2\pi\sqrt{\frac{\ell}{g}}$$

Here $\pi$ is the math constant 3.14 and g is the acceleration due to gravity.

$$g = 32 \text{ feet/second}^2 \ (384 \text{ inches/second}^2)$$

It is interesting that the period of a pendulum depends on the length but not on the mass or weight of the suspended weight.

# Cave Icicles

**Theme:** There are various views of the earth's age.

**Bible Verse:** But, beloved, do not forget this one thing, that with the Lord one day is as a thousand years, and a thousand years as one day. (2 Peter 3:8)

**Materials Needed:**
- Baking soda or Epsom salts
- Paper towel or thick string
- Three glasses (two large, one small)
- Water

## Bible Lesson

Our verse describes God's view of time. He is not controlled by the ticking of a clock as our schedules are. Instead, he is completely above the limitations of time. In fact, God can look down upon history all at once, from the moment of creation to the end of time. Time began at the creation week as a framework for our daily lives.

Sometimes 2 Peter 3:8 is used to imply that a long time period passed during the creation week. In this view, each creation day was actually a thousand years or much longer. However, the verse context is not discussing creation. Instead, it declares that what might seem to us to require a long time can be accomplished quickly by the Lord. The entire creation *could* have been completed in six microseconds or it *could* have taken six trillion years. However, in the literal view of Genesis 1, the creation week covered six normal days. After all, the creation account is the origin of our calendar week. Evidence for long ages—such as radioisotope dating and star distances—all have alternate interpretations. Our science activity will explore just one of these supposed evidences, stalactite formation in caves.

## Science Activity

Many of us have visited underground caves. Unusual formations found there include stalactites hanging from the ceiling and also stalagmites growing upward from the cave floor. These stone "icicles" grow as minerals are left behind by dripping water from the cave roof. It is often assumed that stalactites require thousands or even millions of years to form. However, stalactite growth depends on many factors, including cave humidity, temperature, air circulation, the rate of dripping water, and mineral content. When conditions are ideal, cave formations may develop rapidly.

Miniature stalactites can be grown over a period of several days. First, fill two glasses more than half full with either baking soda or Epsom salts. The Epsom salts make a more realistic stalactite. Then add warm water to the height of the powder in each glass. Stir the solutions to dissolve as much powder as possible.

Twist a paper towel or thick string to make a rope-like cord about 12 inches long. Place the ends of the cord in the glasses and let the center hang downward between the glasses as shown. Liquid should

Miniature stalactites can be grown on a wet paper towel.

creep along the towel from both ends and drip off the center. Place the smaller glass under this drip. Over several days, a small stalactite should form near the center of the towel. When the center glass fills with drip solution, it can be poured back into the large glasses.

The leader may want to grow some stalactites ahead of time to show the group. Materials could then be given to participants to take home.

## Science Explanation

The two alternate chemicals suggested are baking soda, $NaHCO_3$, and Epsom salt, $MgSO_4 \, 7H_2O$. Both dissolve readily in water. Capillary action causes the liquid to move along the paper towel, which acts similarly to a wick. Then as the water evaporates, the chemical is left behind to form a growing residue.

Cave formations are typically made of the minerals calcite, $CaCO_3$, or quartz, $SiO_2$. These natural stalactites are much harder and more durable than our homemade stalactites. Stalactites have sometimes been observed to form very rapidly. They have been found wherever there is seeping mineral water, for example in mines, the basements of buildings, and under bridges. When derived from concrete, the mineral formations often consist of calcium hydroxide, $Ca(OH)_2$, rather than calcite, $CaCO_3$. The hydroxide material is typically soft and flaky. Ongoing creation research demonstrates the rapid formation of the hard, solid $CaCO_3$ form of stalactites as well, under ideal conditions.

Many cave formations probably grew rapidly in the centuries directly following the Genesis flood. For many years there was much mineral-laden water moving underground. The slower growth noticed in most modern caves is probably on a greatly reduced scale from the earlier, rapid growth.

The conclusion is that cave stalactites and stalagmites do not prove the earth is ancient. Many scientists believe that the earth was created just a few thousand years ago. Many present-day cave formations may be a testimony to the floodwaters of Noah's time.

# A Perfect Balance

**Theme:** Don't be knocked off balance by false teachers.

**Bible Verse:** You therefore, beloved, since you know this beforehand, beware lest you also fall from your own steadfastness, being led away with the error of the wicked. (2 Peter 3:17)

**Materials Needed:**
- Potato or ball of modeling clay
- Two metal forks
- Pen or pencil

## Bible Lesson

There are many false teachers in the world today. Jude 13 calls them "wandering stars," those who do not provide a good example or proper direction. The believer must be on guard so that he or she is not misled by those who do not truly represent the Lord. In our day they may be found everywhere: in churches, on television, and in books. False teachers can be a great hindrance to faithful servants who are truly serving God. By their misdirection such teachers keep others from receiving the gospel. They may also cause believers to lose their balance and their testimony. The best way to detect error is to thoroughly know God and his Word. A positive example is provided in Acts 17:11, where the Bereans examined the Scriptures daily to see whether or not the messages they heard were true.

## Science Activity

Objects can be balanced in several unusual ways. The drawing shows that a potato or ball of clay can easily be balanced on a pencil point. What is needed to make this work is some weight suspended below, provided in this case by the two forks. You might pretend the feat is difficult at first, then show that anyone can easily support the potato by a single point.

The balanced object can be compared to the Christian life. Mature Christians are not easily led astray or knocked off balance. Instead, even when swayed by temptation or trial, their lives quickly return to a stable upright position before God.

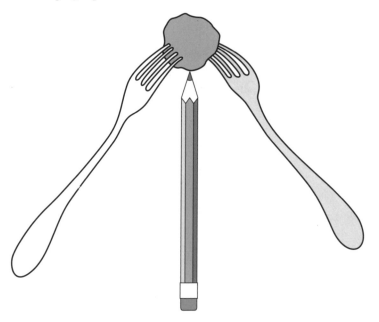

Objects can be balanced in unusual ways.

## Science Explanation

For an object to balance as shown in the drawing, its center of gravity or balance point must be located beneath the top point of support. This will be true for the potato or clay if the two forks hang downward. With practice, the potato can be made to rotate while balanced.

# The Wonder of Water

**Theme:** Water displays God's creative handiwork.

**Bible Verse:** Fear God and give glory to Him, for the hour of His judgment has come; and worship Him who made heaven and earth, the sea and springs of water. (Revelation 14:7)

**Materials Needed:**
- 9-volt batteries
- Paper clips
- Salt
- Small clear containers of water
- Tape

## Bible Lesson

The book of Genesis tells us that God made everything, including the land, the seas, and the heavens above. All things were made supernaturally, from nothing, by God's mighty word:

> For He spoke, and it was done;
> He commanded, and it stood fast. (Psalm 33:9)

Try as we might, we simply cannot comprehend how God created the universe. As Deuteronomy 29:29 explains, "The secret things belong to the LORD." The supernatural is in God's realm alone, being by definition *outside* of nature. For this reason, all attempts to fully explain the origin of the universe, the earth, or the beginning of life itself are futile. In the science world, natural origin theories rise and then fall again, only to be replaced by the latest new theory. Perhaps we should simply praise the Creator for his work and not attempt to understand exactly how he accomplished it.

In studying the present-day creation, we can see some of the building blocks that God used. For example, our verse describes the water that fills the vast seas and that bubbles from the ground as springs. This common chemical called water is not just a simple, formless liquid. Instead, it is made up of two separate elements, hydrogen and oxygen. In the creation of water, God formed these two elements complete with their electron, proton, and neutron components exactly in place. The details of chemistry and physics also were established during the creation week. It is easy to read Revelation 14:7 without giving much thought to the infinite details that were actually put in place. The words from Scripture truly reveal a mighty God.

## Science Activity

This activity can be done by small groups. Water is divided into its component elements, hydrogen and oxygen gases, by using *electrolysis*. This is the name for the electrical separation of the components of any chemical compound, in this case water.

Two partially straightened paper clips are attached with tape to the terminals of a fresh 9-volt battery. This is the common type of rectangular battery used in devices such as smoke detectors. Avoid touching the paper clip wires together since this "short circuit" may result in a rapid heating of the wires. However, there is no serious shock hazard with a small battery.

Dissolve a pinch of salt in a small, shallow container of water; the exact amount of salt is not important. This salt will help the water conduct electricity. Now lower the straightened ends of the paper clips into the water. As the chemical reaction begins, many small bubbles of hydrogen gas should appear around the wire attached to the negative terminal of the battery. The other wire probably will not bubble, but instead will slowly darken as oxygen combines with the metal of the paper clip. By using a clear, shallow container, the bubbles rising from the water electrolysis can be seen.

The battery provides the needed energy to divide the water into its component elements, hydrogen and oxygen. Because the atoms are tightly bonded together, water molecules do not ordinarily break down in nature. Even in the form of steam, water is still stable. God made water molecules to be a permanent blessing for the earth.

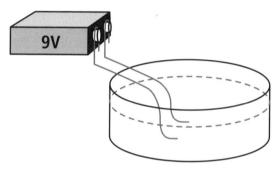

An electric current from a battery will break water down into its component elements, hydrogen and oxygen.

## Science Explanation

Many compounds can be divided into smaller components by using electrolysis. The reaction for water is

$$2H_2O \rightarrow 2H_2 + O_2$$

The hydrogen gas is readily seen forming at the negative battery terminal. The oxygen atoms combine with iron on the surface of the paper clip to make iron oxide, FeO:

$$2Fe + O_2 \rightarrow 2FeO$$

If one uses a larger battery or several small ones connected together in series, then enough oxygen may be liberated to cause visible bubbling from the positive battery terminal also.

# Water of Life

**Theme:** Water is a precious natural resource. How much greater is the gift of salvation!

**Bible Verse:** And the Spirit and the bride say, "Come!" And let him who hears say, "Come!" And let him who thirsts come. Whoever desires, let him take the water of life freely. (Revelation 22:17)

**Materials Needed:**
- Plastic sandwich bag
- Water
- Candle and lighter

## Bible Lesson

Water is the natural resource most often mentioned in Scripture. In biblical times, people living among the dry hills of Palestine knew the value of water. In Scripture water symbolizes the Holy Spirit and also the new birth (John 7:38–39). Consider some of the parallels between water and salvation:

Both are priceless yet free.

Both are available to all.

Water is essential for physical life; salvation, for eternal life.

Although the gift of salvation goes far beyond the temporary, refreshing benefit of water, physical water provides a constant reminder of the life that Christ has provided for us.

A plastic bag with water in the bottom will not melt if placed directly over a flame.

## Science Activity

Water possesses many unique and beneficial properties. It is the only chemical that exists in three different forms at earth temperatures: solid ice, liquid, and vapor or humidity. All three forms of water are essential for a healthy earth. Other unusual and important water properties include its dissolving ability, surface tension, and expansion.

This particular activity shows the large heat capacity of water. Liquid water is able to absorb and give off immense quantities of heat. In this way it moderates the temperature of the entire earth. The moon, with no air or water, has a daytime temperature of about 200°F (93°C), dropping to −200°F (-129°C) when in darkness.

Begin this activity by asking the audience what happens when a plastic sandwich bag is placed in a flame. Most people have watched hot plastic quickly curl up and melt away. Tell the group we will try this experiment, but first we will add water to the bag. Fill the bag with about a cup of water and light a candle. Now hold the bag directly in the flame, making sure that the flame contacts only the water-filled portion of the plastic. Move the flame back and forth along the bottom and the sandwich bag will blacken. Still, the plastic remains secure. This activity can actually be continued until the water boils. Once in a great while a small pinhole leak will occur in the bag.

The activity shows how water is designed with unusual heat-holding properties that keep the earth's temperature comfortable. Water is a gift that is valuable in many other ways besides for quenching our thirst. Likewise, salvation is a gift that we cannot fully understand but should certainly appreciate and accept.

## Science Explanation

This activity shows water's unusual ability to store a large amount of heat. This physical property of materials is called heat capacity. Here are some comparative values of heat capacity for various liquids:

| Substance | Heat capacity (calories/gram·°C) |
|---|---|
| Acetone ($C_3H_6O$) | .506 |
| Ethyl alcohol ($C_2H_5OH$) | .54 |
| Liquid mercury (Hg) | .033 |
| Sulfuric acid ($H_2SO_4$) | .27 |
| Water ($H_2O$) | 1.0 |

Water, with a value of 1.0, has the largest heat capacity in this list. The physical properties of water and other chemicals are not accidental but designed by the Creator for our benefit.

**Don DeYoung** chairs the Science and Math Department at Grace College, Winona Lake, Indiana. He enjoys teaching Bible and science truths to children and adults, using hands-on activities whenever possible. While at Grace College he earned the McClain Teaching Award. Dr. DeYoung is a graduate of Michigan Tech and Iowa State Universities. He holds a PhD in physics and also an MDiv from Grace Theological Seminary and serves as president of the Creation Research Society. He is the author of twenty books on Bible and science topics. Don and his wife, Sally, have three married daughters and nine grandchildren, a ready group of participants for Bible-science activities.